An Exploration into Graphic Design

An Exploration into graphic design

Hong Yin Sun

Arbor Hill Press, Fredericksburg, Virginia

Library of Congress Control No.: 2005928069

Sun, Hong Yin
    An Exploration into Graphic Design/Hong Yin Sun
    ISBN 1-890156-10-8

Graphic design: Hong Yin Sun

Contents

Foreword

We are exposed to examples of graphic design every day – at the local news stand, along the grocery aisle, on billboards and posters, on the sides of coffee mugs, and in business mailings, to name only a few. Graphic design exerts a subtly pervasive influence throughout our daily lives, yet we are rarely mindful of its capacity for persuasion at the moment of influence. If the graphic designer has accomplished his marketing goal, we have grasped the message, selected the recognized brand name, learned about the event, purchased the sale item—all the while quite unaware of just how we came to make these particular consumer decisions. Good graphic design integrates itself into the visual culture so seamlessly that we are never completely cognizant of its presence or of its power to affect our decisions.

At one time or another, each of us has experienced a piercing insight which seems to have come to us from out of nowhere. This experience of enlightenment can seem almost mystical because of the suddenness of its appearance and the astonishing clarity of the insight. Young designers experience these insights regularly as they work to solve one design challenge after another. They may like to believe that these insights and the process of arriving at a design solution is somehow mystical. Because this process seems mystical, beginning design students often believe that the process that leads to this enlightenment is not open to in-depth analysis and investigation.

Hong Yin Sun's years of designing curriculum and supervising instruction in Higher Education have equipped her to dissect the subject of Graphic Design into easily comprehended fundamentals and then to reassemble them into an integrated totality. Understanding the inner workings of the discipline cultivates mastery without subtracting the magic. In fact the opportunities for "magical" insight are amplified as the designer acquires insight into the complex interdependence of the various components. The resulting magic then serves to stimulate the young graphic designer's enthusiasm rather than obscure their vision.

Likewise, Hong Yin Sun has brought her background experience in fine art, art history, art education and design to masterfully demystify the principles and processes which the designer must negotiate in order to create a beautiful work of graphic art. The layout of this book reflects her logical, and practical, approach to designing by organizing the text so that every other page alternates between a discussion of aesthetic theory and a presentation of practical design issues. Theoretical discourse is reinforced with examples of actual design solutions in the graphic designer's arena of activity. In this way, theory and practice reflect their contrast, interdependence and involvement—the main themes of the book.

Gerard Huber
Professor of Art
Texas A&M University-Commerce
Commerce, Texas

Preface

Graphic design has played a very important role in human society since its origin. It is important not only because of its functionality in *visual communication,* but also because of the beauty that it has added to everyday life. Tracing back to the cave artists' paintings, tracing back to the pictographs of ancient Egypt and China, and looking at graphic design from the view of a member of the information age, we have found *graphic design* both functional and aesthetic. Although the graphic design pioneers, the cave artists, and their audiences, might pay less attention to its aesthetic values than to its communication purpose, graphic designers today achieve effective communication through an ideal unification of *functionality* and beauty. The design idea and the technology-enhanced means of design are the wings of modern graphic designers; they enable the designers to soar in an unlimited space of creativity.

In the early stages of art and design history, people did not see a big difference between *graphic design* and *fine art.* Even in the prosperous period of ancient Greece, people still thought that sculpture and crafts were the same. They saw more differences between the media of creation, such as painting and sculpture, rather than differences between fine art and practical art. As art and design developed through the ages, graphic design was eventually considered to belong to the category of practical art. This is based on the fact that there are differences between graphic design and fine art, because a work of graphic design, unlike a work of fine art, is created for certain clients in order to communicate certain information or to send certain messages to the audience. And the message should be transmitted as clearly and strongly as possible. It is not enjoyed as "Art for art's sake."

There are some distinctions between graphic design and fine arts in general. Graphic design tends to be more direct because its attention is to communicate a clear message, whereas fine art tends to be more indirect because it is focused on aesthetic feelings. Graphic design tries hard to meet the client's needs because every production of graphic design is designated to a special client area, but fine art emphasizes the expression of the artist's inner world. Therefore, graphic design tends to be rational, but fine art is basically sentimental and expressional. As a graphic designer, you may have many purposes of design. You might design for yourself, but for most occasions, you will design for your clients and design for the viewers of the situation in which you are interacting with your clients.

Effective *visual language* of graphic design contains indistinct beauty when it is communicating certain messages. Some messages are even transmitted through the use of image ambiguity and hence provoke *aesthetic feelings.* This is the beauty of graphic design. This kind of beauty exists in both graphic design and fine arts. Therefore, there are common characteristics in both graphic design and fine arts. Just like any other type of art, the style and correspondence of an artist or designer play a significant role in graphic design. Graphic designers are artists. Graphic designers can never be "designing machines" that lack of artistic characteristics and styles. Artistic *styles* are the artists and designers themselves. Based on this belief, there is no distinctive difference between graphic designers and fine artists. Some artists, such as Austrian artist *Klimt* (1862-1918) and American artist *Whistler* (1834—1903), are both designers and artists. In the United States in the 1980s and 1990s, designers such as *Carson* (b. 1956) started expressionism in design.

However, the *functional* characteristics of graphic design have determined that graphic design belongs to the category of a practical art. Many client areas build up limitations and conditions for graphic design practice. If clients commission the designers to design advertisements for their products, the designers would not start creating at their own desire and interests without learning the products and *analyzing* prospective consumers of the products for their consuming behaviors and their art taste. Graphic design is an art form that exists for a variety of purposes, such as informing, advertising, and influencing.

The graphic design *procedure* may be quite lengthy and detailed, but there are certain major steps which can be identified. The procedure is a somewhat orderly process entailing a number of sequential steps. In addition to analyzing the audience, the designer should define the design *problem*, or figure out the main point of the design task. Then, the designer works to form a *concept* that leads the whole design. When there is a concept present, the designer can start working on the initial drafts, maybe from *thumbnail sketches*. Finally, the designer goes into the last stage of finalizing the design. This stage includes having conferences with clients, making the final touches, and printing or producing the design product. These steps can be applied to the solution of various design problems, though each individual designer might have a slightly different approach to solving a particular problem. Design decisions should be based on the designer's understanding of the purpose and problem of the design task. He or she will need to engage in a phase of *research* before the design starts. Design history is rich, and there are so many designers around. Just reviewing the designs that have solved similar tasks helps you to discover why those problems are solved that way.

This book helps you discover the beauty of graphic design, understand graphic design elements, and use principles of graphic design. It helps you get started with the most primary elements of design – point, line, and shape. Gradually, it leads you to explore more complex concepts and practices of graphic design. This book is based on the belief that graphic design, just as all design types, ideas, and components, can be described in terms of three kinds of relationships:

Contrast: In the relationship of contrast, two design elements or qualities, for instance, black and white, appear in opposite positions. Just as Chinese philosophical thought has pointed out, any thing has two opposite aspects; and the two aspects together build up the balance. Yin and Yang, heaven and earth, mountain and water, sun and moon, male and female, black and white, brightness and darkness, etc., are all pairs of contrasts. When something is seen larger, it is compared with something that is smaller, and vice versa. Contrasts compose an important principle of graphic design.

Interdependence: In the interdependence relationship, two design aspects or qualities, for instance, form and content, depend on each other and complement each other. None of the graphic design components or images can exist without the other components. *Form* and *content* in design are two aspects that cannot be separated. Content has no way to display without form; form has nothing to depend on without content. Also, no elements of graphic design can be isolated from other elements; nothing in graphic design is absolute; and no single design principle can exist without the existence of other design principles.

Involvement: In the relationship of involvement, two aspects or qualities of design, for instance, *unity* and *variety*, involve each other. One concept, one element, or one image is always involved within another; and concepts, elements, and images involve each other. All details belong to a whole. Therefore, absolute details do not exist. The same is true with regard to human beings in experiencing *infinity*, because infinity is composed of, or involves, numerous moments.

The design elements, together with the properties of contrast, interdependence, and involvement, make the relationships and principles of graphic design. This book would like to serve as a beginning point for you to discover the beauty of graphic design, to understand elements of graphic design, and to use principles of graphic design. Toward this end, this book has its content arranged as follows:

The even pages of the book are devoted to the main concepts of graphic design, mostly with regard to the principles and aesthetics of graphic design. The odd pages, except for chapter title pages, introduce various client areas of design and demonstrate the design and technical considerations in designing a certain client area through design examples, because graphic design can serve many different communication needs. At the end of this book, there is a content map that provides you with an outline and guidance in the following aspects of graphic design:

- Elements and their properties
- Principles and rules
- Aesthetics and procedures
- Areas and productions
- Techniques and tools

Graphic design is a wonderful world that needs all who love it to explore, experience, and enjoy it. It also needs our hard work to make it even more amazing in the future.

Hong Yin Sun, Ed.D
Muskingum College
csun@muskingum.edu
http://muskingum.edu/~csun/

Acknowledgements

A sincere and special expression of appreciation is extended to Dr. Donna Edsall, Professor of English at Muskingum College, for her effort in editing this book and for her encouragement during the writing process.

I gratefully acknowledge the gracious support provided by Art Professor Gerard Huber of Texas A&M University-Commerce for endowing me with his insight and for writing such a thoughtful foreword for this book.

My husband, Yan Sun, and our son, Xiao Mark Sun, are my greatest support and my constant inspiration. Without their support, the publication of this book would not be possible.

chapter one

PERCEPTION

Music is composed using musical notations. Whether it is a magnificent symphony or a graceful serenade, both are composed of those same basic music notations. Graphic designers have their own notations as well— *graphic design elements*, but we will see that the meaning of these elements differs from one designer to another. Designers are working on a two-dimensional *space* and are manipulating the design elements in a meaningful way. Among the many elements of the graphic design language discussed in this book, three elements - point, line, and shape - are the most essential ones. These design elements compose every graphic design project; and each project has its own unique way of using these design elements.

Points are very small units of design. A point provides the potential for a whole design and gets the design procedure started. As design elements and language, points can be used to create independent designs. Most methods that are visible include the use of points to form the outlines of a shape (Figure A) and the use of points to create *volume*, by varying the frequency and size of the points.

Figure A. Point

Many points can be connected to form *lines*. Therefore, lines involve points. You can use lines to define objects by drawing the contours (Figure B), representing the texture of surfaces, or even creating an artistic atmosphere or emotion. Works by British illustrator *Beardsley* (1872-1898) show how the designer uses lines not only in depicting figures but in expressing emotion as well.

There are lines, both *visible* and *invisible*, in graphic design. Visible lines are the ones that are physically visualized in a two-dimensional space, like the contour of an object, for example. There are also invisible lines in the composition that help the audience to capture the flow of information and its hierarchy. These are called "*implied lines*." They are invisible because they are not physically drawn in the design. Rather, they are formed through the organization of visible elements (P.24 Figure A).

A *shape*, in design, denotes a unit of the primary elements in a big construction. Think about a circle, a square, or a triangle. These are simple *geometrical* shapes. Shapes can involve both lines and points. Lines can appear as the contours of shapes and can also be used to create the surface, volumes, and texture of shapes. In addition, various shapes can be created through an inspirational

Figure C. Shape

moment in nature. When shapes are based on familiar objects and keep the original objects recognizable, they are *representational* (Figure C). Sometimes, shapes can be very *nonrepresentational*. Although some shapes are based on known objects, they are transformed and conceptualized so much that they become *abstract*. Appreciation of designs based on abstract shapes needs our insight according to our experiences, feelings, and *association*.

Figure B. Line

A product, a company, or an organization needs to be visually recognized through a *visual identity* system. This system basically includes a logo, *stationery* set (business card, letterhead, and envelope), *advertisement*, signs, and other publications. In a broader sense, this system also includes environmental and interior design, costume, and *exhibition*. All the elements in the visual identity system are unified by standard colors and fonts. *Logo* design is the center of visual identity design.

Before you start designing a logo, you must first decide which type of logo you want to design and if it best fits the client's needs. Of the many logo design approaches, several options are open to your decision-making: type-based or font-based, such as the IBM (1956) logo by Rand (1914-1996); font or realistic and representational visual combination, such as Girl Scouts logo by Saul Bass & Associates (1978); or font and abstract form combination, such as ABC logo by Rand (1965). The logo type you choose will influence the route you take with the logo design procedure you choose.

The most effective approach of logo design is to reach a high abstraction. To be *abstract* is to minimize the design elements needed, but only to a degree that the logo can be recognized immediately, can be remembered easily, and can be reproduced at any size without difficulty. Photos usually are not a common choice for logo design.

When you are designing logos, use vector-based graphic software tools rather than bitmap based tools. *Vector* images are object-oriented images, and the different parts that compose the image are independent objects. A series of anchor points joined by lines define the images mathematically.

Color, shape, and line are all self-contained entities. It is very easy to modify individual objects or change the size of them. *Bitmap* images, in contrast, are composed of an array of little squares called *pixels,* the smallest element of an image or the smallest element a screen can display. Resizing a bitmap image, especially to make it larger, will cause loss of image quality.

The *Multicultural Education Seminar* DOT *Site* logo simply takes advantage of "StopD" font to efficiently transmit the idea of link, which is both the mission and medium of an organization that offers multicultural education seminars over the Internet. Though a type-based logo, the letter "i" is made pictorial to symbolize "enlightenment" by adding the red color and halo, whereas its typographic details are maintained. See pages 5, 23, 37, and 39 to view how this logo appears in various other products of *MES* DOT *Site* visual identity system in enhancing the visual image of the organization.

Positive and Negative Space/Shape

Using space is such a big topic and such a major part of graphic design that it is one of the most challenging tasks that every graphic designer works with. A graphic designer works on a two-dimensional *space*. Imagine you have a blank sheet of paper in front of you. That is your working space. When you introduce images and type on the design, then space is occupied. The occupied space is usually called *positive space*. And the space that is not occupied is usually called *negative space*. Let's take "*This Is Your Link,*" a folder design on Page 5, as an example. The space where the red Chinese ornamental knot and the titles appear is positive space, and the unoccupied background is negative space. You recognize the image and the words because of the *contrast* between them and the background. The relationship between negative and positive space contributes to the *balance* of the whole design, and you always need them both because they inter-depend on each other and complement each other. The background makes the image and type highly recognizable, and the image and type fill the background with meaning. From this example, you understand that "negative" space plays a positive role in graphic design. Therefore, don't try to occupy every single space of the design with images and text.

We can further explore the positive vs. negative issue by examining positive and negative *shapes*. Look at the Yin and Yang symbol (Figure A). In this symbol of the wholeness of universe, Yin is represented with black and Yang is represented with white. Yang is the *negative shape* and Yin is the *positive shape*. The interesting thing is, just like the physiological idea indicated by the symbol itself, you cannot configure Yang without Yin and you cannot perceive Yin without Yang. That is because Yin and Yang are complementary shapes that share the middle contour. You are not able to recognize the positive without the negative. Therefore, "negative" shape, just like negative space, is in fact an "active" shape which plays a positive role in graphic design.

According to *Gestalt* psychology, a theory of visual perception originated in Germany in the 1920s, visual perception comes from organizing and grouping sensual forms following principles of *similarity*, *proximity*, *continuation*, *closure*, and figure/ground. The *figure/ground* principle indicates that we perceive a figure or shape that is on a ground or background. The figure or shape is usually the occupied space and the background is usually the blank space. However, sometimes, the blank space itself is a shape, too, like the shape Yang in the symbol. This kind of design employs a reversible figure-ground relationship. And because various types of figure/ground relationship can occur in design, positive and negative spaces not only contrast each other and complement each other, but also involve each other. Please notice how Yin has a little bit of the Yang and Yang has a little bit of the Yin in the symbol. *Involvement* of a little opposite quality makes each side more balanced. We add *varieties* to a *unified* design in order to make it eye-catching.

Figure A. Yin and Yang Symbol

Folders, or presentation folders, are handy promotional tools to hold and organize loose paper, business materials, and sometimes, objects. In a promotional effort, folders can be mailed to or handed to the target audience. Their flexibility and functionality make them a favorable choice by companies and organizations. Think about what can be held in a folder – business cards, letters, information sheets, worksheets, annual reports, flyers, advertisements, brochures, CDs, small product samples, manuals, and other office tools – you name it. A professional-looking folder is more likely to be kept by the audience, and, most likely, the materials that it holds will be kept as well.

A folder, in its simplest format, is a flexible cover folded in the center and used as a holder for loose pages. But folders often are designed to have inside pockets that make it easy for materials stay stably inside the folder. Also, business cards and CD slits are designed to give the card a nice display in the folder.

As with other *visual identity* designs, folders have aesthetics attributes, in addition to their flexibility and functionality. Design tasks of a folder include front, back, inside spread, flap, and pockets. As a presentation tool, the *logo* should be given first consideration on the folder. At most, the design needs a proper location for the logo on the front. Folder designing is very challenging because multi-function inserts are expected inside. Think about how you would display the loose pages in the folder in order to give audience a quick impression of what's inside. Various colors and sizes can be applied to the loose pages, as the *Multicultural Education Seminar DOT Site* folder design shows.

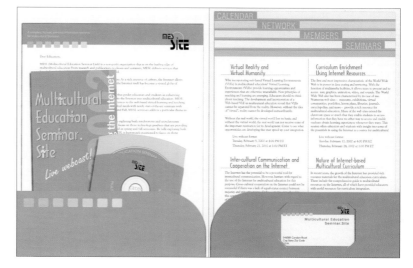

The *Multicultural Education Seminar DOT Site* folder is 9 by 12 inches in size, the typical size of folder design. The organization logo appears in the lower right-hand section of the front. The red Chinese ornamental knot *contrasts* with the light background. The idea is to use the knot to indicate the mission and goals of this organization – the promotion and sponsoring of multicultural educational activities via web links. Its inserts include a letter from the organization, a business card, a brochure, a CD, and loose pages.

Form and Content

To *visually communicate* is to effectively communicate certain messages through visual elements and representations, such as colors, shapes, symbols and signs, photos, motion pictures, and visual expression of linguistic signs. The key components are the visual cues, the center of the *visual language*. Visual communication products can evoke an *aesthetic feeling* that is characterized by an artistic sense of beauty. Form and content are two aspects of the *whole* of visual communication. It is difficult to discuss form and content separately because they are really in a continuum. There is a difference, however, concerning which aspect of that continuum is reflected by form or by content.

What is the message you wish to communicate? *Content* represents the sense and meaning of a graphic design work, a production of visual communication. In a narrower sense, content is the information, linguistic message, the symbol, the hint, the latent meaning, and the intention of the design.

How is your message transmitted? Some type of visual appearance, style, or delivery is needed for the transmission. Design *elements* are needed for the transmission. *Form* is the quality of design that gives a clear arrangement and appearance of the design. Form gives the pattern and helps channel the communication. It is the means by which the meaning is communicated. Although form is based on *content,* it also complements and enhances content, because it establishes the physical existence of content. The solidity of form ensures the visualization of the content. Without form, content will have no place to stay visible.

People *see* designs through forms and *know* content when they view a design. Form has its relative independency in art creation. Effective forms are likely to be connected to the enhancement of contents. The *interdependence* of form and content gives you an idea of how form and content, just like Yin and Yang, will seem to contrast each other when they are separated deliberately. However, they are in fact inter-depending on, or complementing, and *involving* each other.

A *book cover* gives the audience the first impression of the book. Although book cover design sometimes might be simply thought of as merely an "add on" or decoration of a book, it is gaining more and more attention from graphic designers and publishers alike, because the cover and the contents of the book are increasingly considered to belong to the "oneness" of the book. A book should have a cover when it is produced. Every book has a cover. An attractive book cover design does not only communicate the information of the book, but can also enhance the communication procedure.

A typical book cover design includes three parts: a front cover, a spine, and a back cover. Book sizes are from big, such as folio (12x9 inches), quarto (9½ x12 inches), octavo (6 x 9 inches) to small, such as quadragesimo-octavo (2½ x 4 inches) and sexagesimo-quarto (2 x 3 inches).

Book cover design needs a design *concept*, or initial idea. The formation of a design concept is based on the designer's understanding of the contents, and requires that the designer be familiar with the story or characters in the book. With that in mind, the designer can start thinking about the format, color, and images, as well as the production procedure. Sometimes, the spine and front cover are of equal interest in the design. It is important because whether the books are in a bookstore or at home, they usually are put on bookshelves and, if the books are not spiral bound, the readers see the information on the spine first. Designing a book spine needs to include considerations of the thickness of the book and paper weight. It usually requires more than 60 pages in order to make a book spine visible.

The book cover design, *"Educational Technologist – a Concise Handbook and Working Model for Training Effectiveness,"* uses dark blue to create a depth and to set off the title and subtitle. It also uses the blue to create a high-tech, academic look. The *repetition* of a mouse image, with a little hue adjusting, facilitates an illustration of the contents. In this design, both a stately academic atmosphere and a pleasing practice experience are reflected through an impressive feeling that is enhanced by the lighting effects.

There are two aspects involved in the discussion of "horizontal" and "vertical," which is an orientation issue. One aspect is the format, and the other is layout.

Format is essentially related to the orientation of design. It determines the composition and the first visual impression of the whole production. Except for designs that render equal width and height, many design tasks require you to make a decision on whether you should work in a horizontal format (Figure A) or a vertical format (Figure B). Making such a decision will need consideration of the purpose and function of the design.

Figure A. Horizontal Format

Further, we need to think about the *design elements* in the selected format, and the arrangement of design elements, or the *layout* of a design. Usually, *horizontal* lines in a design create a sense of stillness and stability while *vertical* lines create a sense of the potential of movement. These kinds of feeling, to a great extent, come from the imperceptible influence of our natural environment.

If vertical *lines* suggest potential movement, we can go a step further to make them diagonal lines. Draw a picture in your mind: a perfect vertical line is standing straight, right in the middle of a design. Imagine this vertical line is a tree. Then a strong gust of wind is blowing. The vertical line, the tree, becomes a diagonal line. The wind is pushing the tree, and the tree is bouncing back. A *tension* or visual force is created in the composition. Tension adds dynamism to graphic design.

Figure B. Vertical Format

Look at the design "*Red Door*" on page 13 and Figure A. This seemingly quiet and still scene is full of constant changes. That is because of the tension created by the diagonal lines of the steel structure. Such a movement or change is not an actual *movement*, but a reaction to the *compositional* capacity. It is about how to give the design or page an overall arrangement.

Of course, different feelings brought by horizontal or vertical arrangements are relative. Many graphic design works will not be confined to "either horizontal or vertical" myth. Rather, they combine both horizontal and vertical lines in one design, just like all the forms that Nature shows us. Some designs have a composition that have an intricate intersection of horizontal and vertical lines as well as horizontal and vertical *implied lines*. In addition to horizontal and vertical lines, design composition can use other kinds of implied lines to guide the viewer's eyes through the design — circular lines, zigzag lines, or wriggly lines.

Just as with other client areas, *calendar* design is both functional and aesthetic. Its function involves a table-like design that systematically divides time according to months or weeks of a particular year, and it organizes the pages in an efficient way. There are various types of calendar design. The most common designs are wall calendars, desk calendars, and single-sheet calendars. Among these calendars, there are promotional calendars and art calendars. Promotional calendars feature products or services. Art calendars feature paintings and photography. Subjects of art works could be architecture, landscape, flora, or people. Art calendars can be promotional calendars, too, for both commercial and non-commercial purposes.

In addition to the basic information of a calendar, such as year, months, weeks, and days, the designer should also consider highlighting traditional, national, and international holidays, as well as special event days, if the purpose is to promote or advertise. For multi-page 12-month wall calendars and desk calendars, the designer should think how to keep the *consistency* of the design with regard to theme, color scheme, font family, and grid. *Grid* means using lines to structure the layout design. The most commonly seen grid system resembles dividing a page into columns, but various lines, such as diagonal lines and curve lines, can also be used for a grid. The *theme*, or subject, decides the whole artistic atmosphere, and the *layout* decides the ease of navigation.

If you are designing a 12-month calendar that has each month on a particular page, remember to include small tables of the previous month and the subsequent month on the page of the current month. For example, it would be very helpful if you included February and April tables on the page of March.

2006

AUGUST

Most modern calendars mar the sweet simplicity of our lives by reminding us that each day that passes is the anniversary of some perfectly uninteresting event.

Oscar Wilde

	sunday	monday	tuesday	wednesday	thursday	friday	saturday
			1	2 Special Holiday	3	4 Strategy Day	5
	6	7	8	9	10	11 Strategy Day	12
July	13	14	15	16	17	18 Strategy Day	19
	20	21	22	23	24	25 Strategy Day	26
September	27	28 Conference	29	30	31		

Romantic Charm of Studios The Southeastern Interior Designers Association

The calendar design, *"Romantic Charm of Music Studios,"* is promoting an interior design studio. Each page of the calendar, from the January page through the December page, features a particular studio interior with its unique style. However, all the pages fall into the consistent layout *unified* by the grid system.

There are various ways in which visuals, colors, spaces, and verbal components can be harmoniously distributed and blended together in order to complete a powerful *composition*. The principle of such distribution and *hierarchy* is called *balance*. There are a variety of balance systems in graphic design. We often distinguish among kinds of balance by speaking of symmetrical balance, asymmetrical balance, and radial balance; what characterizes these three types are the distribution of visual and verbal elements upon which they are built.

If you ever see a design that has a mirror of form on opposite sides of a centered dividing line, or axis of symmetry, you are most likely seeing a design that is in *symmetrical balance*. Symmetrically balanced compositions are interested in creating an impression of high stability, solemnity, and formalization by visual equilibrium. Symmetrical balance can generate extraordinary power and can have lots of potential (Figure A).

Figure A. Symmetrical

Figure B. Asymmetrical

Most of the times, you might see a different way of arrangement other than a symmetrical balance system. That is, although the design presents the beauty of a pleasant composition, it doesn't have the kind of equivalence possessed by symmetrical balance. This balance system is called an *asymmetrical balance* system. An asymmetrical balance system provides feelings of movement, energy, and aliveness (Figure B).

In order to give the composition a harmonious look, you have another choice. The last of them is very different from either the symmetrical or asymmetrical balance systems. It doesn't have a center dividing line in the composition which allows you to make the opposite sides identical or different; rather, it has a center point that allows elements in a design to radiate and move around it, thus creating a special balance system – *the radial balance* system (Figure C).

Figure C. Radial

Many graphic designers have a strong sensation for form; their good use of balance system can enhance the intrinsic strength of a design. Good symmetry, along with *repetition* of color, shape, or other design elements, imparts *rhythm* in a design. Although many compositions are asymmetrical, symmetrical, or radial, many other compositions fall into something that is not clear-cut. Which balance system is most efficient depends on the purpose of the design and the designer's style.

It should be pointed out that referring to asymmetrically balanced composition as "unbalanced" composition is inappropriate and mistaken. Every design should be very well balanced, but not necessarily symmetrically balanced. A symmetrical balance system might involve asymmetrically balanced compositional elements. Instead of restricting the balance discussion to certain balance systems, graphic designers pay more attention to compositional balance. *Compositional balance* is basically what Arnheim (1974) mentioned as perceptual equilibrium and could be in any of the above balance systems, or in one that has a non-clear-cut balance system. The eye's "intuitive sense of balance" plays an important role.

An annual report, a multi-page design, is an integrated part of a financial and public relations approach. It is part of the visual image of a company, a manufacturer, or a non-profit organization. It not only contains the company's financial reports, but also its identity, strategies, goals, and objectives.

Contents of an annual report may include a letter from the president of the company, special events, accomplishments and innovations, decisions, financials, directors and officers, donors, and so forth.

An annual report design should emphasize both legibility and creativity. *Legibility* means being concise, clear and understandable. *Creativity* means being eye-appealing and attractive. Charts and graphs are very efficient tools for financial, sales, and marketing sections. Photos can provide a feeling of personally being on the scene. And illustrations are very good to help explain concepts and terms. Selecting visuals for the annual report is based on the contents. There should be a close relationship between visual content and verbal content.

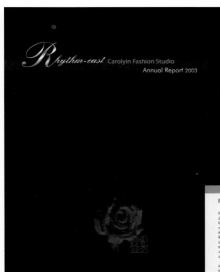

The "*Rhythm•East Carolyin Fashion Studio Annual Report*" uses the corporation standard color (dark blue) and image (blue rose) for the cover design. It is in *consistency* with other visual identity designs such as an advertisement (p. 15) and a shopping bag (p. 35), as well as a poster (p. 45). The format of the cover is *vertical* and in an almost *symmetrically* balanced composition. This arrangement not only keeps the *harmony* of the whole design, but also helps impart confidence among clients. As a public relations tool, this design emphasizes the clarity in content presentation. The page layout uses a lot of blank *space* that guides readers through the document.

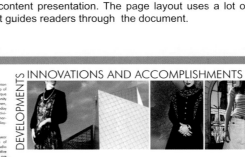

Fashion and Style

Founded in 1989 as a ladies' fashion design studio and company by a group of fashion professionals who studies unique needs and interests of a fashion community that is composed of working women, Rhythm-East Carolyin Design Studio today is providing a wide range of designs, activities, and presentations. This year is a marvelous year of Rhythm-East Carolyin in playing an important role in the trend.

Major innovative design projects in this year have provided the chief constituents of Rhythm-East Carolyin Design Studio success. Extraordinary design, innovative technique, and high-quality materials are critical to the proper functioning of any fashion design studio. These capabilities span the entire Rhythm-East projects and they are among its core considerations. With today's emphasis on new but reminiscent feeling of fashion, there is an increased demand for high-quality designs. Whether shimmery silk dress or textured cashmere sweaters, Rhythm-East Carolyin makes a simply but luxury image that belong to a collection forever. Our customers need us to develop a passion for femininity, and by combining grace, elegance, and chic, Rhythm-East Carolyin has created a style that not only adds beauty to women's life, but also adds confidence in themselves. •

Runway Highlights

As a result of the collaboration from Rhythm-East multi-disciplinary team consisting of designers, strategists, and engineers, designers of this studio, Ouyang Ling, Ma Yao, and Ma Jin, have made waves in the fashion community.

Tong Fantasy Gala featuring evening wear was held at the Cheng Huang Miao auditorium in Lanzhou. The show opened with shimmying silk downs, and most of these were restructured out of their Tong grace with exaggerated belt loops. The stage became a bridge that links the past and the present for Lanzhou's fashion followers, as it showed how a limited space could reflect the whole sense of history. Our designers took the opportunity to reveal their new collection of graceful blue series. And there was a sea of blue to choose from.

For Spring/Summer 2001 Fashion Month in Linton, we showed our Silk Road series designed by Ma Jin and Ouyang Ling. It was time for the fashion community to embrace a new approach to dress, a new feeling, new choices, and new opportunities. In all the presentations during the month, we have the perfect combination of a beautiful collection and a enlarged audience. The elegant environment of Rhythm-East exhibition set the mood for a series of distinctive fashion shows in the future. •

DEVELOPMENTS

INNOVATIONS AND ACCOMPLISHMENTS

Interactive Fashion Online

By combining innovative ideas, high-quality products, and web design expertise, Rhythm-East Carolyin Design Studio has created an interactive web site that not only let women notice the latest fashion trend, but also give them the chance to use their imagination. The highly interactive design allows users to work on their virtual wardrobe - select dresses and accessories, then create the best arrangement for themselves. The website, www.rhythmeast.com, is the online promotional vehicle for this growing design studio. •

Trade Exhibition

The Rhythm-East Carolyin Design Studio Trade Exhibition from April 28 through June 20 had enhanced trade relations with southwest China and had created numerous business opportunities. It involved many designers, manufacturers, and businessmen to find the best of almost everything come from Rhythm-East Carolyin Design Studio. •

Over 500 fashion business visitors of southwest China attended the exhibition to seek new designs and opportunities. The success, both in terms of sales and commercial endorsements, presented the promise of this unique design studio. This also represents the fact that Rhythm-East Carolyin Design Studio has become an integral part of the growing fashion business. •

Designers

Congratulation to designer Ma Jin for being awarded the First Price at Spring/Summer 2001 Fashion Month! Ma Jin's blue diamond evening dress with pleated skirt is just one of the exciting examples that keep fans looking forward to each new collection. This dress scores points with its simpleness and the fantasy come from deep ocean and shiny sky.

Designer Ouyang Ling made a decision on black and white modernism while Ma Yao started a new line on white suede jacket. Both of their efforts are emotive and the models are on point with the harmonious chic. •

The digital image on page 13, "*Red Door*," shows a fantastic view. In this design, a girl with romantic charm, together with an impressive steel structure, constructs a powerful visual influence. The sharp *contrasts* among quality, weight, size, and *space* of these two very different visual items make this design an appealing work.

Steel is heavy. The *weight* of steel sets off the floating robe of the girl. The fish is even lighter than the robe. We find out these weights by comparison, and this kind of weight comes from our knowledge of the physical weight of the objects. But in a graphic design, there is also the compositional *weight* which establishes the *compositional balance* of a design. Other than the physical weight, this kind of weight is determined by an object's position in the composition, the object's relationship it has with other objects, and the object's color. Therefore, in this digital imaging design, it is the fish that plays a significant role in keeping the balance. The fish is "heavier" than it is in a normal sense.

Figure A. Outdoor

Figure B. Desktop

Weight is also related to size. *Size* refers to the dimensions of an object in design. And size, just like weight, is relative. Figure A and Figure B both show you the same exact Nike sculpture. However, you would believe the sculpture in Figure A is a huge outdoor sculpture and the sculpture in Figure B is a desk decoration. This is because you refer to the sculpture's background information while determining the size of it. If the sculpture is represented alone in a photo, you cannot tell its size. The size of the sculpture in the first example appears big because its background is a city scene. The size of the sculpture in the second example appears smaller because it is put in front of a globe and some books.

Contrast in size can be used in graphic design to create visual interest. It can also be used to decide the right *proportion* of a design. When we speak of size, we are talking about the dimensions of an object itself or the design itself. If we further discuss this object's relationship to the whole design, or we discuss the relationship between objects with regards to size, we are discussing proportion. In the digital imaging work "*Rhythm of Life*" on page 25, you see a dancer in good proportion. That is, her head is roughly equals to one eighth of her body, the belief of perfect proportion of human body espoused by the ancient Greeks, defined as the golden mean.

The spatial relationship with regard to size among the dancer, the ship, and the globe creates a very attention-grabbing structure. This dancer image takes the right amount of space in the design, and the design establishes a very efficient way of using space. It not only ensures the streamline-like link of the objects in this design, but also guarantees enough blank space of the layout. If the dancer were too big, it would make the design too busy. If the dancer were too small, it would not be strong enough to impact the audience.

With new technologies coming, the graphic design world has entered a digital world. *Digital imaging* refers to the concept, process, and techniques of using electronic devices and computer software programs to create and manipulate images and digital photos.

Digital imaging covers the use of computers to transform images, to alter colors, and to build images based on information from various other images. It can also create surrealistic images, add special effects to images, change image layer blend mode, paint and draw, and so forth.

Methods of digital imaging depend on the features of software programs. The most commonly used methods include selecting necessary *pixels*, copying/ cutting and pasting, and applying filters (built-in image manipulation functions of a computer program). *"Red Door"* shows a young lady unbelievably walking in the air. She is an unreal person created through the use of a combination of graphic software techniques. The sky background is created by transforming a digital photo of sky and clouds, so it is full of *motion*. Other digital photos have been used for the steel structure and the mysterious fish, a nice ocean suggestion.

Creating digital imaging work requires your *imagination*. Although sometimes you can get unexpected but excellent outcomes from trying some graphic software features, you need to learn the features and have the ideas in mind when you start.

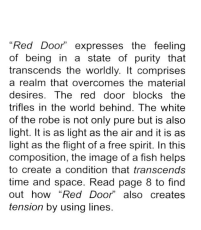

"Red Door" expresses the feeling of being in a state of purity that transcends the worldly. It comprises a realm that overcomes the material desires. The red door blocks the trifles in the world behind. The white of the robe is not only pure but is also light. It is as light as the air and it is as light as the flight of a free spirit. In this composition, the image of a fish helps to create a condition that *transcends* time and space. Read page 8 to find out how *"Red Door"* also creates *tension* by using lines.

Black and White, Light and Shadow

Although graphic designs can be blazing with millions of colors, a black and white solution is still the first option of many designers. It is not only because of the lower expenditure of producing black and white designs, but also because black and white, just like in the realm of fashion design, are two colors that never become obsolete.

First, a *contrasting* use of white against black or, vice versa, can enhance the design's overall strength. Just as the Yin and Yang symbol shows, pure black and pure white are at two extremes. The darkness and brightness are shown in their full status. They are so pure that the audience can enjoy simple and unadorned lines or shapes.

Second, the various grays or *shades* created by linking black and white emphasize the charm of light and shadow. And light and shadow can be used to create a sense of *depth* and a sense of *volume*. Figure A shows how the different grays are applied to a circle and the circle appears as a three-dimensional object, a ball. The audience almost can tell that it takes a certain amount of space. Light and shadow, both in black/white and color designs, can also be use to create a deep and mysterious atmosphere. In art history, Dutch painter *Rembrandt van Rijn* (1606-1669) and French painter *La Tour* (1593-1652) are artists whose artistic styles are characterized by unique ways of using light and shadow. Many graphic designers have also used light and shadow to increase the touching effect. For example, the poster "*Federazione Italiana inks,*" by *Dudovich* (1899-1900); the poster "*Safety angle – 4 up – I out,*" by British designer *Games* (1947), and the poster "*Für das Alter,*" by Switzerland designer

Vivarelli (1949), all show ingenuity in using light and shadow.

Third, the various grays themselves represent rich visual effects that allow the audience to appreciate the dreamy atmosphere in the composition. Black and white photos attract many audiences because of the simplicity, nostalgia, and enhancement of shapes and lines.

Fourth, black and white can be combined with a certain hue or color to create a tonal depth for a *monochromatic* design or monochromatic effect in a design. That is, the design is based on only one hue, with variations of value. In order to create monochromatic effects, a hue must be selected. *Hue* refers to the quality of a color by which it can be perceived. Let's take the advertisement, "*Your Collection Forever,*" on page 15 as an example. Blue is selected as the basic hue of the monochromatic effect. The black and white are then added to the blue to change its *value,* or its range of lightness and darkness. Adding different amounts of black to the blue creates different *shades* of the blue; and adding various amounts of white to the blue produces various *tints* of the blue.

A monochromatic approach is most often used to develop a highly *unified* look of the design. It also creates a depth that gives the audience space for their imagination and experience.

Figure A. Light and Shadow

Advertisements are designs that focus on informing people about products or services, convincing people about the quality and effectiveness of products or services, or reaching out to the *audience* attention about the products or services.

There are some key components in an advertisement, including a main image or visual, a main advertising sentence or verbal message which provides more information about the products or services, contact information, as well as company's logo and catchphrase or motto. Advertisements can be smaller ones, such as those in magazines. They can also be huge ones, such as those on billboards along the highways. They can be anywhere.

The process toward achieving advertising goals involves an *analysis* of the audience and the development of the main design idea and concept. Some of the design problems associate with sales, whereas some of the design problems associate with public service.

Advertisements are one of the most popular client areas of graphic design. People see advertisements everywhere, and those advertisement designs are competing. This makes advertisement design a challenging task. In order to attract the audience, novelty of using color, layout, and verbal message are expected in all advertisement designs. One of the best ways to get an objective view of your ad design and your other designs is to imagine that you are the audience and assume the audience's response to the designs.

Designing advertisements not only needs inspiration in order to have exceptional insight but also needs enthusiasm to create a sensational look. The advertisement designed for Rhythm·East Carolyin Fashion Studio, "*Your Collection Forever,*" uses an almost *monochromatic* arrangement to enhance the harmony of the design. The gesture and the silver lines create a great *tension* in the composition that raises the *emotional* response from the audience. The *repetitive* appearance of the blue rose − the company's symbol flower − together with the flower image in other promotion designs, helps establish the company's visual identity. As an advertisement of a lady's fashion design studio, it emphasizes gracefulness and imparts a sense of high quality.

Details exist in a design for the sake of wholeness. Being *whole* is the life of a design. Being separable literally, details and wholeness can never be separated in reality. Being whole involves details seamlessly in a design. A design might contain fabulous details; however, they must always yield to the whole and should never distract the audience.

Sometimes, a new designer might be engaged to details and finally find that the audience was so attracted by the details that they almost ignored the main message of the design. The details were taking the whole away.

The concept of "Whole" suggested by *Gestalt* psychology can help us to understand more about the relationship between details and whole. According to Gestalt psychology, we perceive any visual images through an organizing process of our perception system. This organizing procedure gives us a whole form of the image, but not the details. As a result, the sum of details doesn't equal to whole, and the whole cannot be divided. The whole determines the details. When the *audience* is viewing a graphic design, they perceive the details or the relatively independent visual elements. However, if the audience obtains a strong visual cognition, that is not because of unrelated details or design elements, but because of the inter-relationships and interactions among the elements.

A detail in graphic design has no real significance until it takes its place in the composition of design as a whole. Therefore, a graphic designer must possess a supreme method to achieve a satisfying wholeness of the design. More often than not, in a design work, some parts are simply more important than others. Arrangement of the parts needs great effort. Various parts in a design can be ordered in a hierarchy of descending importance. *Hierarchy*, in graphic design, means categorizing visual and verbal information into levels according to their relative importance and then giving them proper position and *size* in the layout. Every detail in the design should have the right size and should be in a proper *proportion* with the whole design. Color and value should also be considered. Good hierarchy of both visual and verbal information can give *emphasis* to the design and can create a *focal point* or a big attention getter in the design. The focal point is the same as the climax of a melody of music. This focal point assumes greater importance than the rest. A good hierarchy also helps to maintain the audience's interest in the design.

Another powerful method of maintaining the wholeness of a design is creating rhythm. Having *rhythm* in a design means to have the regular repetition or pattern of certain design qualities and elements, such as color or shape, to aid in creating a *movement* or a harmonious flow in the whole design. The *TaoCarolyinRiver Juice* packaging design on page 17, as a series of packaging designs of a variety of juice flavors, can be perceived as whole, though every one has its details. That is because this series has created a whole impression or atmosphere by using the lively, healthy-looking color scheme of green, yellow, and orange. Although each flavor has its own images, the *grid* is the same. The details are all determined by the flow of the "*TaoCarolyinRiver Juice*" melody.

Packaging design is both 2-dimensional and 3-dimensional because most package designs are created on a 2-dimensional *space* and are eventually applied to 3-dimensional packages for products, such as tools, food, beverages, and cosmetics. It is expected that the fascinating design of the package plays an important role in "alluring" consumers to buy the products.

Packaging designs in their finished forms are boxes, bottles, cases, and bags, etc. The juice cartons on this page and the CD cases on pages 37 and page 51 are all packaging design examples. As "containers" of various products, packaging designs are utilized to protect products efficiently, to store products safely, to transport products easily, and to advertise products effectively. Materials for packaging range from softer types, such as paper and plastic, to harder types, such as glass and metal. At times, a graphic designer will need to cooperate with other parties and stimulate a variety of innovative ideas.

As an integrated part of *visual identity* and branding, packaging design is the most "*functional*" among other designs. The designer needs to have a definite object in view. Ease of use and safety of use should be considered in the design procedure. Other factors involved are material characteristics, capability, recycle ability, mechanics, and so forth. Packaging design usually includes logo, product image, function explanation, open directions, bar code, and other related information.

In addition to functional considerations, the designer's greatest effort is on how to give the product a high-quality look. A high-quality look not only gives consumers a deep impression of the product, but also enhances their confidence in the product.

The "*TaoCarolyinRiver Juice*" series focuses on how to give the product a "healthy" look. Yellow, yellow-green and orange colors are *associated* with heath and visually ensure the quality of the juice. Although the same *grid* and color is repeated on the carton of each flavor, realistic images of fruits are used. And images of each kind of fruit are shown in three aspects: the whole fruit, a section, and juice in a glass.

As a considerable component of *visual communication*, *graphic design* products transmit messages visually. Whether you are designing a brochure or designing a small label, if the purpose of the design is more than aesthetic needs, it will almost certainly contain a message. This is because graphic design is a *functional* art and its function is to convey messages visually. By providing information through the arrangements of images and words, the designer helps the audience understand and memorize the message of the design.

A design is a whole *visual message*. We can discuss the message in three aspects or layers.

The observable aspect of a design contains images, also referred to as the *visual;* and words, also referred to as the *verbal.* Usually, the images are considered visual because they are expected to be seen; and the words are considered verbal because they are expected to be read. All these are based on a consideration of the distinguishing quality of images and words.

In the second aspect of a design, both images and words are considered visual because they are all immediately perceived by the audience as images at a certain degree. They are the main components of the *visual language* used by graphic design. Visual or verbal messages are based on the visual appeal in order to affect the audience or viewers. Since words are also considered visual, there is the theory and practice of *typography.* In the earlier ages of graphic design, typography is the subject that studies printing with movable type. Now, typography represents the creative use of type, that is, to arrange and manipulate the letters and numbers available in various *type families* (Figure A) that have unique *typefaces* (Figure B).

Graphic Design

Graphic Design

Graphic Design

Graphic Design

Figure A. Type Families

ABCDEFGHIGKLMNOPQR STUVWXYZ

abcdefghijklmnopqrstuvwxyz

1234567890

Figure B. Typefaces

Many factors can affect the outcome of type use in addition to type families and faces: *size* (the scale of type); *style* (regular, bold, italic, or underline); *leading* (space among a set of text lines); *tracking* (space among a set of characters); *kerning* (space between two characters); and *baseline* (the invisible line that helps characters line up vertically).

In the third aspect of a design, the message is considered as a circumstance in which the designer, the message, the media, and the audience and their response, all form a circle of correspondence. The *audience's* active and conscious thoughts formulate the understanding and retaining of the message by processing the images and words intellectually. The visual message of the design becomes more "verbal" in the audience's mind.

The *World Wide Web* (WWW) is a browsing and searching system that allows an audience to access information on the Internet in a sequential or non-sequential manner while viewing web pages – screens that display hyper-textual integration of text, graphics, animation, video, and sounds.

Designing web sites requires teamwork among programmers, graphic designers, system administrators, and writers. A web site typically contains a homepage, some core pages and their sub-pages. Each web site has its unique address, or *URL* (Uniform Resource Locator). A URL looks like this: http://muskingum.edu/~csun/

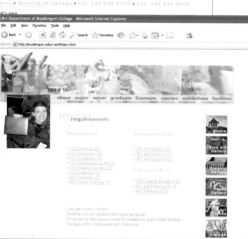

index.html. Or a short-hand URL http://muskingum.edu/~csun/, can be used in this case because "index.html" is a default home page filename. A web page contains both visual and verbal information, as well as links to other pages. The links are "hot" text that audience can click to evoke another page to display. The growth of the Web demands creativity in *web page design*.

There are various ways of creating web pages. The primary method is to write with html (HyperText Markup Language) codes or tags. However, html editors, software programs that allow you to create web pages in a WYSIWYG (what you see is what you get) working environment, are much easier and faster. Web graphics are created in *RGB* color mode in order to display on screen in w*eb browsers*, software programs designated for viewing web pages. The most commonly used graphic formats for web pages are GIF and JPEG. GIF stands for *Graphics Interchange Format*. It is effective for compressing diagrams and no-detailed images. JPEG stands for *Joint Photographic Experts Group*. Many Web browsers can display this format, which is effective for compressing large, color image files and for detailed images.

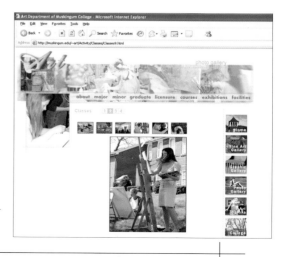

A web page designer should try not to leave any page as a dead end, that is, no links to go any where from the page. And a designer should not ignore broken links, the links that are no longer active. The "*Muskingum College Art Department*" web site is designed to deliver information about the department, such as course offerings, activities, exhibitions, and an online art gallery. Its clear, simple, and consistent navigation system allows an audience to easily find information on this web site. The *harmony* and *unity* of the site is maintained by keeping the *consistency* of colors, image styles, layout grids, and typography. The relationship between the images and contents of the pages is emphasized.

T his chapter provides you with information about the elements and components of visual language in graphic design. Mostly, it introduces the perceptual aspect of design and it answers the question of "what you see" in graphic design.

This chapter also involves a discussion about design procedure. Effective graphic designers follow planned steps or consistently used steps to complete a design. Although the steps are discussed one at a time, good designers do not go through them as separate steps – they move back and forth among these steps. Through the design areas introduced in this chapter - logo, folder, book cover, calendar, annual report, digital imaging, advertisement, packaging, and web page design – you have learned that the major steps involved in graphic design procedure can be identified as analyzing the audience, defining the design problem, forming the design concept, working on sketches, and finalizing the design. In the following chapters, you will read more about how you can create designs that are not only functional, but also emotional through creative approaches.

chapter two

SENSATION

Graphic design consists of various *design elements:* point, line, shape, space, and color.

Colors are recognized by *hues:* red, yellow, blue, green, pink, etc. One color has various *shades* that can be used to create depth. Colors also have higher or lower *saturation* because of diverse levels of purity. We also refer to this kind of color attribute as *intensity*.

Figure A shows a *color wheel*. It is a system or device that helps us to study and use colors. This color wheel is based on the three *primary colors:* red, blue, and yellow. They are primary because you cannot use other colors to create them, but you can use them to produce other colors. As the color wheel shows, when two primary colors are mixed, a *secondary color* is produced. Orange, purple, and green are three secondary colors. Further, when a primary color and a secondary color are mixed, you receive a *tertiary color*. Orange-red, yellow-green, and purple-blue are some examples of tertiary colors.

Very often, we also refer colors as cool or warm colors. In the color wheel, the colors ranging from the yellow-green, yellow, orange, to red seem warmer; and colors ranging from blue-green, blue, to purple seem cooler. Comparing the "*MES DOT Site*" brochure on page 23 with "*Rhythm·East Carolyin Fashion Shopping Bag*" in page 35, you will feel the colors of the brochure warmer and the colors in the shopping bag cooler.

Temperature is not an inherent property of colors. We understand that feeling of temperature is based on sense. Many feelings, such as cool and warm, can be obtained through physically touching an object. The sense communicates the temperature of the object to us. But we don't physically touch colors when they are displayed on computer screen or are printed on paper. We have a simulated or virtual touch using our eyes.

How can touching colors by our eyes let us feel cool or warm? It is made possible by our previous experiences. It is a psychological phenomenon. It is *color association*. The fire is warm and the sunshine is warm; therefore, when we see bright colors of fire and sunshine, such as orange or yellow, we associate them with fire and sunlight. The same is true with the cool color of the blue sky and ocean water. Whether a color is cool or warm also depends on its contrast with other colors. Cool or warm is relative. For example, pink might be felt as cooler than red.

Cool and warm colors can be used in a design to create an artistic atmosphere and *emotional* condition that gives the audience a strong impression. Usually, using warmer colors is related to energy, warmth, health, excitement, and vivacity; and using cooler colors is related to peace, tranquility, sentiment, comfort, and mystery. But all these are relative. A light purple might suggest romance, whereas a dark purple might imply grief. Therefore, a designer will need to consider how the factors of value and intensity of color can affect the use of warm and cool colors.

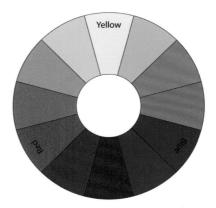

Figure A. Color Wheel

Brochures are used widely for promotional purpose. They are small informative booklets or pamphlets that introduce and advertise products or services by using the flexibility of the cover through detailed information, both visual and verbal. There are different ways in which a brochure can be printed and folded. Common folding methods include the accordion fold, the gate fold, the tri-fold, and the parallel fold. An accordion fold (Figure A) refers to parallel "Z" folds. The gate fold (Figure B) consists of four panels, and two of them look like the two panels of a two-door gate. The tri-fold (Figure C) has three folds. And the parallel fold is similar to tri-fold, but it has one more panel.

Many brochure design projects, especially those intended to be used for presenting detailed information, probably involve a large amount of text, along with various types of images, such as photos, illustrations, and graphs. Because a brochure is a two-side design and will be folded, it requires more consideration in page *layout*. How do you want to fold the brochure? Where will the "cover" of the brochure be? The *Multicultural Education Seminar DOT Site brochure* is a parallel fold brochure with 8 panels. Therefore, each side of the design, side A or side B, is divided into four columns or panels. The left two panels of side A serve as the front and back covers of the brochure.

Notice how the colors and images are printed so they seem to go off the edge or edges of a page? That is called *bleeding*. In the production procedure, any color and image exceeding the printable area will be trimmed off after printing, so the brochure is designed about 1/8 inches larger than its final size.

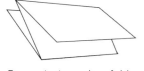

Figure A. Accordion fold

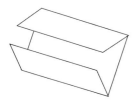

Figure B. Gate fold

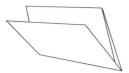

Figure C. Tri-fold

Figure D. Parallel fold

The *Multicultural Education Seminar DOT Site brochure* uses the organization's standard color and font. The letter 'i"s are designed as human images in various colors. This is to symbolize the various cultures and people with various cultural backgrounds in the United States and in the world. They also bring vitality to a formal-looking brochure. The logo appears both on the front cover and the back cover to enhance the image of the organization.

Although it is perhaps hard to imagine creating *motion* in a 2-dimensional, still space, graphic design provides the potentials. This is not a new topic in visual art. *Arnheim* (1974) applied *Gestalt* to the movement of visual art and maintained that *movement* or *motion* is very important to visual art. Just like *Leonardo da Vinci* discovered, if a painting lacks a feeling of movement, it will be more rigid and inflexible.

How do we represent movement in a 2-dimensional space, a still space? It depends mostly on the *tension* and *rhythm* in the design.

Looking at the images, motion can be represented by visible gestures and lines. You can notice this kind of motion in "*Rhythm of Life*" on page 25. The gesture of the dancer suggests a full movement.

From the *compositional* point of view, the tension created by directions and characters of *lines* and *implied lines* create motion, too. In "*Rhythm of Life*," notice how the implied line starts from the boat, passes the dancer's body, and goes through the dancer's right foot (Figure A). This line resembles the line dividing Yin and Yang symbol, and it creates the tension. The lines and *implied lines* are charged with rhythm, flow, and movement in the design. The swirl of clouds in the sky

Figure A. Tension

creates tension also because the two parts have reversing strength.

Sometimes, rhythmical color vibration is also used to create motion. That's why seemingly static forms might contain pulsating energy in graphic design. The tension is generated by the effect of *contrasting* colors. Two-dimensional patterning based on variations of color saturation, intensity, and hue can all create fascinating vibrations. "*Space*" on page 59 gives you a good example of such color-based movement.

Proper use of complementary colors and analogous colors is another way of adding dynamics to a composition. on page 22, you learned about the color wheel. Whenever two colors have opposite positions on the color wheel, they are *complementary colors*, for example, blue and orange. Whenever two or more colors are neighbors, such as yellow-green, yellow, and orange, they are *analogous colors*.

Using complementary colors in a design can create a lively intense vibration. Look at the poster "*Shadow*" on page 45. This design mainly uses cool colors, blues of the sky and water, to create an atmosphere of tranquility. However, bright yellow and orange appear on the background, too. This sparkling area interacts with the blue around it and makes powerful beats in the composition. Using analogous colors in a design most likely creates a smooth and subtle vibration, as shown in the shopping bag design on page 35.

Fluent movements and motion can be created, using lines of various directions, shape *repetition*, and color vibrations. They give the design a seemingly inherent vitality that breaks the limitation of a two-dimensional, or still, space.

Intended to appraise the human life, the *digital imaging design* "*Rhythm of Life*" creates a dreamlike view that represents the globe, the human figure, the sky, and the boat in a very contemporary way. A computer graphics program is used to integrate several photos and a mouse-point-free-hand painting in one. The photos used in this design are digital photos and scanned traditional photo prints. They are rearranged and enhanced with software features.

The background images of the original photos are eliminated. A lighting effect is applied to the dancer to give her a shimmering look. A globe image is created out of textures and free-hand painting. An outer glow effect is applied to it so it seems that the globe is glowing or under a backlight. The clouds are transformed and then twirled to create the reversing forces of wind. This creates the *tension* in the composition. The boat image is copied from a photo and duplicated. The duplicated copy is flipped vertically to create the boat reflection. A flower is distorted and its layer blend mode is changed to have the colors interact with the colors on the layer beneath.

This design also extends the limited space to unlimited space, which can be explained by the law of continuation in design suggested by *Gestalt* psychology. The principle of *continuation* means that when objects form a continuous pattern, we tend to move our eyes through one object and continue to the next, so as to follow an implied direction. Look at the curve line in Figure A of page 24. From where the boat comes, the *space* is extending upward and left. And if you follow the direction pointed out by the foot, the space is extending down and right. This design builds a vision that is not only illusory but also existent.

Topics about whether something is calm or noisy seem to be an issue of auditory sense. However, it is an issue of vision in graphic design. Using visual counterparts, we understand that we hear sounds through our ears. Therefore, we "see sounds" in a design through our eyes. The *harmonious* use of color creates designs that are "calm"; the discordant use of color produces designs that are "noisy."

An in-depth layer of this issue involves the arrangement of ideas in a design. Graphic design uses visual language to impact its audience. It needs to involve the *audience* actively by providing a certain atmosphere in which they can enjoy, feel, and imagine. It is all about creating an artist's conception in design.

From the artistic point of view, a graphic design needs to be encompassed with a prevailing tone or *mood* that is both intellectual and emotional. This is the aesthetic trait of artworks: artistic conception. *Artistic conception* consists interactions between feelings and views. According to Chinese aesthetics, artworks should always pursue an aesthetic feeling that is beyond the depicted scene or objects.

Page 27 shows a digital imaging work, "*Soft Breeze.*" It is calm not only because of its calm scene, but also because of the mental status that can be achieved through viewing it. Calm doesn't mean there is not any sound at all. It means having sounds in the audience's imagination.

The procedure for graphic design establishes the structure in which there is an unvoiced pact between calm and noisy, as well as between others such as clear and obscure. For some design solutions, indistinct and obscure beauty is more likely to raise imagination; putting an object behind a veil is more likely to cause curiosity from people. In some designs, dimming down the surrounding elements of a main image can enhance the main image. This method might create a hazy spatial *depth* that gives the design a more mysterious feeling. The audience can compare the subtle similarities and differences between colors, shapes, lines, and so forth.

Many successful graphic designs do not present the main idea or subject through direct statements. Rather, they use analogy, comparison, metaphor, or figure. The audience is provided with a cue for situating the meaning. In an indirect approach of communication, the meaning is implied. Clear and obscure each complements one another and both are a vital part of design. If a design tries to show everything to the audience, information overload may cause the loss of audience's interest. Usually, a designer tries to use some methods to make indistinct beauty possible.

There are many image sources for graphic design, including *digital imaging*. Most designers will combine various sources in order to create designs of a unique style. The most common method is to use photos, both digital and traditional. To obtain digital photos, you use a *digital camera*, a camera that captures photos and stores them digitally, and that allows photos to be transferred to computers directly. When selecting a digital camera, you need to pay attention to factors, such as resolution, display, focus, storage, batteries, and zoom. Traditional photos can be turned digital by using a *scanner*. Scanners are also used to scan some objects, such as leaves, fabrics, and other relatively flat objects.

You can show your originality by creating images with graphics software programs. Although this option needs time, hard work, and patience in order to master the software features, it gives you the greatest potential to create a style all your own. The digital market knows that one designer, one company, or one organization cannot cover all the tasks of illustrators and photographers, so various stock CDs are available in the market. The CDs contain professional-looking photos and illustrations. Some photo CDs provide designers with photo objects so the designers can use the objects in their designs without too much restraint.

The digital imaging design, "*Soft Breeze,*" uses several digital photos – the sailing ships and the sitting girl with the original background image eliminated, as well as the sky and water with the original photo altered and blurred. This design also uses a stock CD photo object, the church. Various image sources are used to create an *artistic conception* in which the feeling and the scene are interacting and corresponding.

A two-dimensional space or a three-dimensional object both have a topmost material boundary called the surface. Different surfaces will give you different feelings when you look at them or touch them. This is true also in various forms of art. We use the term *texture* in discussing the quality of surfaces that let you experience the feeling of smooth or rough by vision and touch sense.

On page 29, you see an invitation card of an exhibition, "*Reflection and Expression*," that displays two artists' works, three dimensional and two dimensional. Look at the metal sculpture with a rock base. Do you feel the smoothness of the metal and the roughness of the rock? Artist Todd Malenke uses the strong *contrast* in texture as a powerful language for *expression*. If you actually touch a three-dimensional artwork, you will obtain a feeling of the textures directly. If you feel the textures while looking at this printed reproduction, you are obtaining a feeling of the textures by vision.

Look at the photography on the invitation card on page 29 again. Compare the textures of the wall, the skirt, the hairs, the sword, and the skin. Although the contrast of the texture is subtle, you can still find that some textures are smoother than others. In artist Dennis Savage's work, the delicate arrangement of visual elements often adds special attractions.

Texture enriches the *visual language*. Contrast of texture is one of the many effects that build up the impact of graphic design.

Different textures can be used to achieve design goals and to emphasize the subject of the design. Smooth textures are generally *associated* with elegance and subtle emotion; and rough textures are usually associated with strength, determination and confidence. Textures of certain materials can also bring *emotional* qualities to designs. The smooth texture of silk denotes ease and grace; therefore, it is associated to noble and relaxing feelings. However, the rough texture of wool looks warm and simple; thus it is associated with a welcome and an embracing feeling.

You might have heard or experienced how one can get *inspiration* by looking at the clouds in the sky or stains on a wall. Textures can be used to foster *imagination* and to cultivate *creativity*. Take a little stone and stare at it. Does it have the property of texture? Is it smooth or rough? If you feel soothed while touching this stone, try to find out whether you have experienced the same feeling before. If yes, in what situation? Look at the stone, and then try to guess where it comes from. Does it come from a stream, a pond, a creek, or a river? Try to visualize the stream or pond it comes from. Try to visualize the scene as it appears in different seasons or at different times of a day. What are the colors you would like to use to depict the different scenes? Try to describe your feelings as if you are in various scenes. Look at the stone. Does it have a color? Is it white, blue, or red? If you are asked to use these colors to express your mood, which color you would like to use for what kind of mood? … The stone experience can go on and on. It can bring you into boundless imagination and can inspire you for design ideas. To be creative is to be able to see what others cannot. To be creative is to have an original view. Try the texture experiment now.

Postcards are very important public relations tools. They can be used for various purposes: as informational cards, as invitational cards, as advertising cards, or as greeting cards. Sending messages is the main function of postcards.

Various sizes and formats are available for postcards. A typical postcard has two sides: one side is the "front side," where images and verbal messages are printed; the other side is the "back side." It provides the space for return address, mailing address, postage stamp, and barcode, because postcards are sent through the mail.

The great potential of a postcard is in its ability to combine information, and art and culture. It helps in enhancing the visual identity of a company or organization. Nowadays, post offices handle postcards automatically; therefore, the return address should not be put at the location where the post office scans for recipient's address. The bottom part of the backside should be left for the bar code.

"*Reflection and Expression - Art of Todd Malenke and Dennis Savage*" is an invitational postcard for an art exhibition. It uses the artist's works as the main visuals. Both artists are engaged in deep thinking and are interested in using very simple art language to *express* emotion and the inner world. The black background of the postcard sets off the artworks very well and gives the design a sense of *depth*. Gradient effect is used in type so to create a flickering illusion.

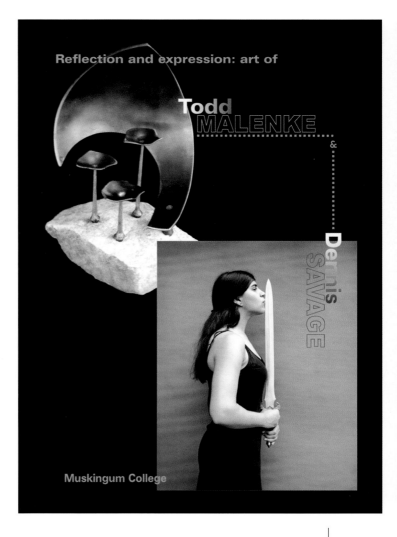

Reflection and expression: art of

Todd MALENKE

&

Dennis SAVAGE

Muskingum College

Strong messages transmit strong feelings. *Emotional* impact is one of the goals of graphic design. Viewing the poster "No noise" by *Muller-Brockman* (1914-1996), the audience cannot help feeling distress between the shock and emotional stirrings. The poster has such emotional intensity that it serves as a powerful tool arousing attention to noise pollution – an invisible destroyer of health.

Graphic design moves an audience emotionally through visual force. Colors, lines, shapes, and tension – all can be used to create an emotional intensity that makes the design moving and touching. Although appreciation greatly depends on individual experiences, many graphic design works can well be qualified as emotional.

Sometimes, an audience's feelings are evoked by the design. Sometimes, the *audience* can register the feelings, negative or positive, to the design and get a certain satisfaction. The joyful feeling or sad feeling obtained from a design not only depends on the designer but also depends on the audience's mood. For example, when people view *Leonardo da Vinci's* "Mona Lisa," it has been found out that whoever is in a happy mood will see Mona Lisa smiling happily and whoever is in a sad mood will feel that Mona Lisa's smile is full of compassion. Corresponding to audience's mental state is an area that is related to the *artistic appreciation* of graphic design.

In art appreciation, association and empathy play a very important role. Sometimes, the audience might have a kind of remembered feeling or sensation that is connected to a certain kind of object, thought, or idea. That is called *association*. Association can happen when the audience finds the connecting point in the artwork. This kind of association seems to lead to very personal appreciation and insights, but because human beings have many common experiences and traits, this association actually leads to a correspondence among a wide audience.

Empathy refers to a two-way *interaction* and reflection between the audience and the artwork. When the audience is viewing the artwork, they can perceive it as something that has feeling, ideal, and thought. In this procedure, the audience members themselves are influenced by the feeling. Therefore, they somehow unify themselves and the artwork as one. In a specific art atmosphere provided by the artwork, the audience obtains aesthetic satisfaction while receiving the stimulating information.

Feelings are not definitive in many situations in graphic design. For example, the fashion design exhibition on page 31 itself does not have a strong emotional expression because of its commercial purpose. However, it is an open space that enables resonance from the audience according to their moods. To those who are in a good mood, this design is encouraging and inclusive; and for those who are in a bad mood, the design is soothing and welcome.

Graphic designers often are involved in some kind of three-dimensional task, such as *exhibitions*. Exhibitions create a visual effect that communicates product information. Exhibitions are decorative and advertising in nature and they are used to promote the visual image of a company. The purpose of exhibitions is to stimulate the consumer motivation.

Exhibition mainly includes exhibition windows and store displays. In both cases, a three-dimensional space is needed for product display, as well as for lighting and scene production. In exhibition design, the three-dimensional space usually has to be divided efficiently, using a variety of materials, such as glass, fabrics, and boards of metal, wood, or plastic. The creation of a scene is significant for setting off the products.

Lighting effect is the key to an exhibition design. First, it can be used to attract the audience in order for them to take a more detailed look of the products. Second, it can be used to create a stunning and dramatic atmosphere in which the audience is influenced imperceptibly but deeply.

The "*Rhythm·East Carolyin Fashion Exhibition*" shows how to use lights. The company's standard color, dark blue, is used to create remote and deep feelings. It sets the tone in this special space, an oasis for relaxation. The dreamy space of this design has no boundary. The spotlights are shining on the models, and thus adding a sense of nobility. The floor is decorated with silk sheets. They are so brilliant and gleaming in the display that they give the audience a vivid impression. This exhibition is an integral part of a larger design scheme, which is the entire *visual identity* of *Rhythm·East Carolyin Fashion Studio*.

Representation and Expression

As a type of *functional art*, a graphic design contains both an informational message and an aesthetic message. Not only do effective graphic designs achieve legibility, but they also try to be more expressive as well, just as fine artworks do. *Visual communication* in its whole form contains *visual* elements, *verbal* elements, and *emotional* elements. Therefore, graphic design needs expression. There are emotional themes at times that become a dominant power in a design.

Representation and expression are two aspects that affect decision-making in composition, typography, image, and color in graphic design. *Representation* refers to the practice of depicting or describing objects, relationships, and scenes in design as they are perceived directly by an audience in the external world. With this approach, objects, relationships, and scenes can be identified by the audience. Representation emphasizes the objective observations.

Expression means to use objects, relationships, and scenes in design according to a designer's inner experiences and emotion. It emphasizes the subjective feelings of the designer. With no constraints of the rational aspect of the objective world, the designers can bring their initiative and imagination into full play. In the expressional approach, visuals might be variations based upon familiar objects, especially when photos are involved; but they usually are not as identifiable as they are in representational approach. The relationship of the external world might be distorted from expression.

Representation and expression are contrasting methods, but they involve each other at different levels. In the process of depicting the external world, the designer will need to go through a selection procedure in which only desired information is used for the reproduction of the objects and relationships. The individuality, tastes, and style of the designer will be projected in the representational approach. As a result, the representation has involved expressive meaning.

An expressional approach can use color and form only, for example, the art for *"Rhythm·East Carolyin Fashion Studio shopping Bag"* on page 35. An expressional approach also uses images and colors based on objective observation of the external world, but transforms or exaggerates them according to expressional needs. As *"in my heart, in my soul"* on page 63 shows, the design is very emotion-dominant and demonstrates how a designer can interpret the subject with a very personal understanding and how a designer can deal with the message by using a very subjective approach without losing the communication interest. In this music magazine design solution, the designer does not use a formal portrait of the musician or the stage photo of the concert; rather, she uses the musician's portrait in an unexpected way. Through the waving reflections in water, there are the bright eyes of the musician, full of passion and aspiration. They open the doors for the audience to reach the innermost being of the artist.

Pole Banner design belongs to the category of environmental graphics and are just one of various banner design solutions in the graphic design world. It adds special attractions to a promotional effort because of its flexibility and its unique way of displaying – being eye-catching in high and conspicuous locations.

There are several basic components of a pole banner installation: the pole, the banner itself, the pole sleeves on top and bottom, and the grommets. Because pole banners are displayed all day long and in any weather condition, the fabric of the banner should be heavy-duty and the ink should be long-lasting. Side binding is needed for the body of the banner.

The overall impact of the pole banner design is enhanced by the method of *repetition*. One banner is only one unit of the banner promotion project. Banners are installed on many poles of equal-distance apart and each unit is displayed on one pole. The background of the banner project is the city scene or sky. Banners are viewed by passing traffic in all directions. In this sense, banner design involves three-dimensional, environmental design considerations.

The *"Plant Green because You Can"* banner is designed for Earth Day global tree planting event of a city and is installed in the main street of the city. Its view in distance, the composition, the color, and the big image are all able to grab someone's attention. Viewing closer, people can be embraced by the atmosphere created by the banners and obtain the message conveyed.

Realistic and Abstract

Graphic designers use a wide variety of sources for their creative work. Visuals used in graphic design range from very realistic images, such as photos or photo-realistic illustrations, to very abstract images such as *geometric* shapes or even several lines.

Realistic and abstract methods give graphic designs contrasting looks: *realistic* visuals are based on observed nature and they depict observed nature; hence, the *audience* obtains a true life feeling. *Abstract* visuals, on the other hand, are based on intrinsic forms; here the audience is able to understand the idea but not identify or recognize objective images and relationships.

Realistic and abstract methods give an audience contrasting *appreciation* experiences: realistic visuals are familiar to the audience because they come from the audience's familiar environment, so an audience can appreciate them based on rational understanding. Abstract visuals are unfamiliar to the audience because they are from the designer's imagination, so the audience will need a re-creation procedure to understand the possibly irrational colors, textures, lines, and forms of the abstract visuals.

Realistic visuals might contain abstract concepts and feelings because they are not always narrative. They sometimes possess indefiniteness like abstract designs. Look at the "*Rhythm·East Carolyin Fashion Exhibition*" design on page 31. Isn't everything realistic? The space, the models, and the fabric are all realistic and familiar to the audience. However, it creates an atmosphere that is very abstract — the *depth* indicates something afar; the models are symbols of elegance; the fabrics form a concept of gracefulness. The audience might find it hard to describe the emotional implications conveyed by this design.

Abstract visuals might cause realistic *emotional* responses from the audience. Sometimes, the emotional world is something beyond what a description can tell us. Abstract visuals, with their characteristics of subjectivity and irrationality, give an audience an unlimited space for their aesthetic association and imagination, as well as for their interpretation according to their emotional needs. While the audience finds the corresponding colors and forms in the abstract design, their emotional reflection becomes more realistic. "*Rhythm·East Carolyin Fashion shopping bag*" on page 35 uses a piece of abstract art. All it has visually are colors, textures, lines, and shapes. Every audience can interpret this artwork in a personal perspective and thus can give it a very different description from another audience.

To sum up, realistic quality and abstract quality in design are two concepts that involve one another. Effective graphic design works can give an audience direct lyrical experiences, no matter whether they use realistic visuals or abstract visuals.

The primary purpose of *shopping bags* is to facilitate consumers in carrying and storing purchased items. But the bags gradually become part of a marketing strategy that serves as means of moving advertisements.

Types of shopping bags range from very simple plastic grocery bags to designer hand bags. They are three-dimensional finished products, so designers should consider every side of a shopping bag design. A common shopping bag is similar to a cube. Usually the opposite sides are identical, but different designers will use different approaches.

Shopping bags are expected to represent the image of a shop or a brand, to imply the quality of the products, to enhance the audience's memory of the shop or a brand, to be part of the culture, and to be a fashion or a part of one's lifestyle. Some shopping bags are designed for special events and have the artist's signatures on them; therefore, the souvenir bags can become collector's items for the audience. Shopping bags are one of the first things to be given away at conferences, trade shows, or open house events. In order to make a shopping bag attractive and impressive, designers try to put lovely images and beautiful patterns on it, plus the *logo* of the shop or brand.

The Rhythm·East Carolyin Fashion Studio promotional shopping bags, with a variety of handle and grommet styles, are made of light-color translucent paper with a subtle textured finish on the outside. Cardboard inserts are applied to the bottom and gussets are applied to each side in order to ensure its rigidity. This design is impressive not only because of its durability, but also its stylish modern look and a breezy feeling. It uses *abstract* art as the main visual and adds the logo on both sides. At its promotional open house event, each member of the audience receives a shopping bag with the designer's signature on it.

Individuality and Generality

A graphic designer has his or her own unique way of observation, creation, and expression, including the use of design elements and motifs. We recognize this *individuality* as an artistic *style*. The heart of graphic design, originality, is reflected in Individuality.

Generality refers to the atmosphere, appreciation interest, or trend in a society. By making a comprehensive survey of art and design history, we can find many examples of how individuality and generality work together to give an impetus to innovative efforts. Graphic design can represent not only the intellectual insights but also the emotional sensitivities of a certain period in a civilization.

Art Nouveau, a stylish decorative movement in visual arts and architecture in Europe and in the United States at the end of the 19th century, is based on the trends brought by the Industrial Revolution. Technological progress and new lifestyles gave artists and designers new adventures and excitement. However, gradual elapsing old customs and fashion made many artists pursue the world of spirit and fantasy. This also reflected the atmosphere of the society and the appreciation interests of their time. As a result, artists and designers created an international art form that fit into the modern age. Artists were guided by the society but still let their art convey a powerful sense of individual style.

Appreciation interest of the *audience* is one of the factors likely to be found on an uncertain background, due to the subjectivity of *aesthetic attitude*. To be aware of and enjoy the aesthetic qualities and values of graphic design, individuals or groups of various socio-cultural backgrounds carry different viewpoints. Graphic designers make the choices that they believe best embody the meaning of the message, according to their tradition and culture. But designers might also influence, even make revolutionary changes to contemporary appreciation interest in a society. American graphic designer *Rand* (1914-1996) not only developed identity systems for major corporations such as IBM, ABC television, and Westinghouse but also developed a distinctive, mainstream American graphic style, a style that is characterized by simplicity and rationality. That is because Rand created designs that embody individuality but are still infused with local culture here in the United States.

One category of packaging design is *CD (*and *DVD) packaging* design. It protects and promotes the CDs, including both music CDs and data CDs. Before the audience can reach the contents in the discs, the only way in which they can obtain an impression of this product is to look at the packaging design – the physical container with images and words printed on it.

The common types of CD packaging include jewel box with tray, double jewel case, C-shell, envelope with window, box with overlay, and paperboard variations.

As with other packaging designs, CD packaging design usually starts with a decision on how this product is going to be distributed. Whether they will be put in retail, given to an audience at a convention directly, or mailed to the audience will end up with very different solutions, in addition to making the design attractive. If they are for retail, think about the way they will be on display. If they are self-mailers, leave spaces for stamps and address labels on the back. And if they are for direct delivery to the audience at conventions, pay attention to their relationship with other promotional materials. Also, CD packaging design, like other packaging designs, will need ecological considerations in order to reduce possible threats of the disposed packaging material to the environment.

The *Multicultural Education Seminar* DOT *Site* CD packaging is one of those paperboard variations. It is to be directly distributed to the audience at conventions with other promoting materials in a big folder (page 5), along with loose page information, a business card (page 39), and a brochure (page 23). This design folds a two-side printing information sheet into a container with a window. Part of the CD is visible, and it is easy for the audience to take it out of the packaging. The color scheme is determined by the organization's standard color and is *consistent* with other promotional materials.

Designer and Audience

A graphic designer's creative work tends to be based on his or her client's practical needs, rather than on his or her own *expressional* needs. In fact, *graphic designers* are often designing in response to a request by clients for certain groups of *audience*. Thus, your design decision is related to the visual, verbal, color, and style; and those rely heavily on the client's needs. Instead of designing what you want to design, you must design what your clients want to use. The best way of reaching the audience is to keep your client's needs in your mind when you design.

An audience can also be referred to as the target audience or the target viewers. They are the direct consumers of the design products. A graphic designer should often explore the "cause (design strategy) / effect (design result)" relationship in order to anticipate and know the expected response from the audience; this helps in designing attention-getting graphic productions. Of course, graphic designers have their own *styles* and their own ways of selecting and using visual elements of design. Designers are working on various solutions in their own manner. That's why the individual nature of the designers can never be erased from designs that address a big population and meet the needs of clients. Graphic designers concentrate on the client's needs, just as they concentrate simultaneously on their primary design interests.

There are many relationships in the designer-audience interaction. *Emotional* response is more important than others because of the immediate visual force generated from the design. Graphic design art can be viewed by its audience in two different ways — as functional art and as fine arts - as functional art with regard to its purpose and as fine art with regard to its form. The audience always perceives the forms and colors before they have an intellectual experience with the design.

Designers and audience are brought up and are living in a variety of cultural backgrounds, so they will have a love of certain designs. For example, color preferences differ from designers to designers, as well as from audience to audience. The American flag is composed of three colors: red, white, and blue. A combination of these three colors in a design will certainly, for Americans, be connected to patriotism, and furthermore, may also be linked to political events and interests.

Many design solutions start with a development of *personas*. A persona is a collective image of a target audience. The idea of persona is based on the assumption that an audience is representative of a group and shares the characteristics, aesthetic interests, lifestyles, needs, and consumer behaviors of other members from that group. Personas should, therefore, reflect the culture and experiences of a particular group. Development of personas helps the audience-*analysis* and decision-making *procedure* in graphic design because persona description provides consuming goals that determine the designer's design goals.

Stationery refers to a series of interrelated designs, including business card, letterhead, and envelope. It is not only part of the office supplies but also a very important component of *visual identity* and is used as a powerful public relations tool.

The common stationery design will incorporate the company or organization logo and contact information in a standard layout. This standard layout is used on all stationery items. Sometimes, conceptual or realistic illustrations are also integrated. It is expected that the layout will reflect the spirit, essence, and missions of the company or organization.

A typical stationery design contains a 2" x 3.5" standard business card, a #10 envelope, and an 8.5" x 11" letter head/writing paper. However, a variety of sizes are available for the designer's choice. Paper stock and color are among considerations of stationery design. Will the stationery be printed in one, two or full color? Will it be printed on recycled, bright white smooth, iridescent, or woven paper? Preferred logo and illustration design are simple and scalable. They should be readable and recognizable even printed in a very small size. Refer to the *logo* design section in page 3 and find out why *vector* images are recommended.

The *Multicultural Education Seminar* DOT *Site stationery* design follows the rule of simplicity, just as other products for the same organization, so to give the three pieces of the stationery a unified appearance and feel. Notice that the logo appears on all the three items, as does the contact information and/or mailing address. The solid color bar gives the designs a very simple look, and gradient color boxes based on the organization's standard color add variety and movement to the design. All items in this stationery design are printed in full color.

Summary

Graphic designers use an aesthetic approach in design. Even with the nature of functional art of graphic design, it is still possible for designers to express themselves through individual styles. This determines aesthetic appreciation within the graphic design. Graphic design can be interesting for its own sake and not as an instrument to some further end.

Elements of design provide a means of clear communication of the message. To understand the emotional impact on audiences, graphic designers should explore possible "cause (design strategy) / effect (design result)" relationships within the design context. This chapter focuses on the "what you feel" question in artistic appreciation of graphic design. Every design work takes on a life of its own.

chapter three

CONCEPTION

In the previous two chapters, you have learned the perceptual and sensuous aspects of graphic design through the relationships of *contrast*, *interdependence*, and *involvement*. From the discussion, you have noticed that the various relationships actually further demonstrate the idea of what is relative or absolute in graphic design. Anything in graphic design that is viewed as absolute, is not. Everything is simply a goal, an ideal, or an impression. Every individual thing in graphic design is relative, although sometimes an item may appear absolute. Each is based thoroughly on relative relationships and can be observed in the following aspects.

In the relationship of *contrast*, a design quality is determined in comparison with another quality. Just as Chinese philosophical thought points out, everything has two opposite aspects; and the two aspects build up the *balance*. Yin and Yang, heaven and earth, mountain and water, sun and moon, male and female, black and white, brightness and darkness, etc., are all pairs of contrasts. When something is seen as larger, that is only because it is juxtaposed with something that is smaller, and vice versa.

In the relationship of *interdependence*, a design quality is dependent on another quality. Design qualities, such as form and content, can never be absolute, independent qualities, though they are discussed separately. None of the graphic design components or images can exist without other components; no elements of graphic design can be isolated from other elements; nothing in graphic design is absolute; and no single design principle can exist without the existence of other design principles. *Form* and *content* in design are two aspects that cannot be separated. Content has no way to display without form; form has nothing to depend on without content.

In the relationship of *involvement*, a design quality is having a connection that unites it with another quality. One concept, one element, or one image is always involved with another; and concepts, elements, and images all involve each other. All details belong to a *whole*. Therefore, absolute details do not exist. The same is true with regard to human beings in experiencing *infinity*, because infinity is composed of, or involves, numerous moments.

In this chapter, the relationships of contrast, interdependence, and involvement will be further discussed while exploring some conceptual areas of graphic design. These areas ask us to view graphic design from a philosophical and aesthetic point of view, and thus we are asked to avoid viewing graphic design solely from its functional characteristics and needs.

As part of visual communications products, *illustrations* are used to clarify or explain content as well as to explain and decorate a text. Effective illustration designs can give messages an informative, pleasing, descriptive, or pictorial visual enhancement; therefore, they can facilitate the audience's understanding and retention of the theme and content.

The area of illustration involves many aspects, such as editorial, advertising, scientific, cartoon, comic, and book illustration. Illustrations can be artistic or technical, or both. Technically, illustrations commonly are divided into line art, continuous-tone black-and-white-art, and color illustration.

Illustration design starts with the designer's understanding of the text or message. Also, training in both studio drawing skills and media-based technical skills is highly demanded. The problem-solving procedure of illustration design needs creativity from the designer that ensures aesthetic and critical achievement of the design. In illustration design, preparation of thumbnail sketches is, as in other design areas, an important step. *Thumbnail sketches* are small scale, less-detailed sketches that help designers to visualize concepts.

The fashion promotion illustrations for the *Rhythm·East Carolyin Fashion Studio* demonstrate how various techniques and colors can be used to enhance the theme. It also demonstrates that on occasions, illustrations are superior to photography because they are infused with the enthusiasm of the designer and his or her unique way of interpreting the trend. Colors, strokes, lines, and lights and shadows all lie behind the innovative design idea. They raise the illustration to a height of chic.

Graphic design is an imaginative art. And a graphic design is a visual appearance of creativity. It might be useful to examine the difference between *imagination* and *creativity,* which is an interesting topic. Imagination and creativity are not equivalent, except in some very special aspects. Imagination is associated to creativity in that it needs the creative power of mind. Creativity is related to imagination in that it shows imaginative ability. Imagination and creativity can be both related to the irrational process and sub-conscious condition of the mind.

In the process of creation, imagination plays a dynamic role because imagination helps in extending the space beyond perception can reach. *Creative imagination* consists of two aspects: First, it enables a designer to structure some mental images that are far beyond what is perceived in a normal way, and thus enables many potentials and possibilities in design ideas. Second, it allows a designer to arrange and manipulate images creatively based on idea, implication, and aspiration. Therefore, creative imagination is central to the aesthetics of graphic design.

Creativity has affinities with imagination and other psychological qualities. Individuals who have creativity usually have high curiosity or experience and are more conscious of what others might ignore in everyday life. They insightfully create various products with originality and expression. Creativity, in graphic design, yields something that is unexpected and thus attractive.

From the store poster on page 45, "*Shadow,*" you will find that the designer gives the common images an uncommon arrangement. This is created in the light of creative imagination in which potential contradictions are explored, re-explained, and visualized. While a girl sitting on the reflection of a bridge is impossible and ridiculous in everyday life, this presentation strengthens the transmitted message of novelty, difference, and fantasy. "*Rhythm·East Carolyin Fashion Studio*" is an own-brand fashion studio that integrates some traditional Chinese philosophical ideas, and it gives emphasis to graceful but impacting styles; therefore, it is appropriate for it to use such a layout to attract people's attention.

To understand imagination and creativity, interior design can be used as another example. Before designers can actually visualize the design on paper or with a computer program, they have to have already formed a coherent picture of a space or particular room in their minds. It is more than what they see in their immediate experience. A calendar design on page 9, "*Romantic Charm of Music Studios,*" contains a series of interior designs that illustrate a variety of atmosphere in spaces. The piano studio emphasizes an environment where music will play a dominant role. The tranquility of the space seems to be waiting for the moment when the music and spirit are unified as one.

In the design procedure, the step of ideation also refers to the formation of innovative ideas that are based on creativity and imagination. The designers are guided by a powerful sense of anything that inspires them.

Posters are large-scale, informative designs displayed in public places. They most likely appear in shopping centers and subways, art and cultural facilities, as well as campuses. No matter what target audience they have, the audience is among the coming and going traffic.

Types of posters vary, depending on the purposes of the activities under promotion. You can categorize them into two big groups: commercial and non-commercial posters. A sales poster belongs to commercial and a public service poster is non-commercial. Every poster design is a product of design art, a visual culture, and a micro-representation of a culture. Posters play a very important role in integrating art into everyday life.

Because most posters are to be viewed from a distance, visuals play a dominant role in attracting the audience's attention and giving the audience a deep impression. Graphic designers will use novel and unusual methods in order to make both visual and verbal messages clean and clear. The center of a poster design is its visual power and visual impact.

The most challenging factor in poster design is the environment. Various posters might appear in the same space, and as a result there is competition. In terms of the poster itself, appropriate visual *hierarchy* is one of the critical aspects. And in terms of the environment, the designer should be aware of possible distractions from other posters.

he poster "*Shadow*" is designed for the *Rhythm·East Carolyin Fashion* *udio* as an indoor poster. In comparison with outdoor posters, this ·sign has a considerable amount of details and a certain tone of color ·cording to the size, the color scheme, and atmosphere of the studio.

Description and Transcendency

You have already read about *depth* in the previous chapters. According to our analysis and discussion of graphic design in perceptual and sensuous aspects, depth has a denotative meaning as well as a connotative meaning. Denotatively, depth is a sense of distance and perceived perspective in a design. Connotatively, depth indicates the intellectual message and profound meaning of a design.

Graphic design is a visual representation of ideas and is supposed to communicate certain messages. In order to achieve that goal, *visual* and *verbal* elements used in a design usually are composed of a *description* of the familiar and known world. This world is what the audience perceives and experiences. It is the culture in which the audience has been brought up. The audience recognizes the images, reads the language, and behaves as expected. Graphic design productions often are made to directly represent the communication subject.

However, a design can *transcend* limitations of time, space, and culture. Though a functional art, graphic design gives designers numerous possibilities to show their inner visions, in addition to many limitations for *expression*. Sometimes, the remembrance is hidden in the designer's inner world for a long time and it reflects thoughts far away. The designer can express the thoughts during the design procedure by making connections and insights in a visual environment. The audience therefore feels something from the design that is beyond the limits of their experience but which still can provide them with aesthetic enjoyment. Of course, these designs often need more audience involvement in order to *interact* with them more efficiently. It is transcendence that gives graphic designs a lyrical, religious quality that is usually thought to belong only to fine art works.

The poster "*Come to Find the Spirit of Tibet*" on page 47 attracts audience attention by a simple layout, a mysterious light, and a tone of color. Both Western and Eastern audiences can be aware of its power because the design uses a visual language that is not confined to a certain culture. It lets the red wall occupy the whole layout and lead the curious viewer to the secrets hidden behind it.

Transcendence is based on a profound conception of experience. Going beyond description not only lets designers enrich their design vocabulary, but also allows the audience to extend their aesthetic experiences.

By comparing this *poster* design, "*Come to Find the Spirit of Tibet,*" with "*Shadow*" on page 45, you will find the differences between an indoor poster and an outdoor poster. Although this design has details, all of them are unified and simplified by a mysterious light. It invites a note of timelessness to the design. The audience grabs the meaning of this design through a deliberately arranged hierarchy – a visual hierarchy that is created by *contrast* of *value*. The flow starts from the word "Tibet" to the full title; then wanders gradually to the windows and the monk; and finally stops at the more detailed information at the bottom of the poster.

Posters are like brochures, stationery, or other printed design products, and they require considerations about printing. On page 19, you learned that web graphics should be in RGB color mode instead of CMYK color mode because they are different from printed designs.

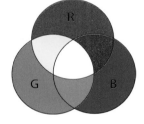

Figure A. RGB

RGB colors are also referred to as *additive colors* because they are mixed by light and display on screens. RGB stands for the three primary colors of additive color – Red, Green, and Blue (Figure A). When red, green, and blue are added together, you get white.

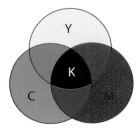

Figure B. CMYK

CMYK colors are also referred to as *process colors* because they are used for printing process. CMYK stands for the three primary colors of process color – Cyan, Magenta, and Yellow, plus Black (Figure B). In the print process, the four colors are not mixed. Rather, color dots made by transparent ink of each color are overlapped to create a full color appearance. Black ink is added to print the darkest area and add depth.

You will need to pay attention to the fact that the printed version of a design in RGB color will have some unavoidable color alterations when converted to CMYK mode. Also, an electronic image in CMYK mode will not be displayed at all or will not be displayed properly in a *Web browser*.

Visible and Invisible

Graphic design is a practice of *visual communication,* and the *audience* experiences the design works through recognizing images, shapes, and type. In the process of communication, there is a sender of the message, the designer, and a receiver of the message, the audience. The design in between informs the audience, raises their sympathetic response, and provokes their actions.

Graphic design has numerous possibilities as a conveyor of meaning. As a kind of art, it has the obvious aspects that are easy to identify and explain; it also has the beauty of ineffableness in various ways which affect the audience cognitively and emotionally. Good designs tell the audience more than what they see. That's why simple compositions can have a profound meaning. This is among the beauty and other artistic virtues of a graphic design work.

With respect to layout, implied line is an invisible quality. On page 2, you learned lines and *implied lines* — lines in the composition that assist audience to capture the flow of information and its hierarchy.

In light of delivery of meaning, visual communication has symbolic meanings of various kinds. Inexplicable as the visuals are, a design can fuse an interesting use of association, resemblance, and revelation, just as a poem does. In the history of the human race, when two things have certain common characteristics or correspondence, one of them is used to *symbolize* another. People automatically associate something with something else. For example, when people see the white robe in *"Red Door"* (page 13), they immediately associate the white color with purity, because white has already been conventionalized as a *symbol* of purity in the Western tradition. Designers also contrive *metaphorical* expressions that make implicit comparisons. Those designs are magnificently conceived and have a poetic vision. For example, the audience senses a metaphor used in *"Your Collection Forever"* (page 15). Sometimes, *connotations* can be used in design to imply meanings behind the visible elements. In the brochure *"Multicultural Education Seminar DOT Site,"* (page 23) all letter 'i'"s that appear in the copy are produced as if they were human images in various colors. This method is used to symbolize the various cultures and people with various cultural backgrounds in the United States and in the world.

Visible aspect and invisible aspect are two contrasting aspects, but they are interdependent on each other, too. Without visible aspects, the meaning has no way to be expressed; and without the invisible, the visible elements have no meaning. It is these *visible,* seemingly limited elements that support all the *invisible p*arts of the design — the consequence occurred after the *interaction* between the design and the audience. Here the graphic design is trying to make the meaning conceptual and to locate it outside of design. Therefore, we can also say that the invisible aspects are involved in the visible aspects of design.

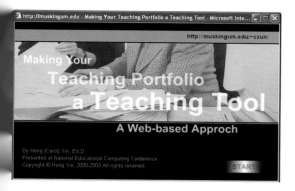

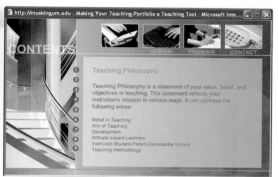

Interactive instructional designs include classes, lessons, tutor als, manuals, tests, and other teaching and learning materials posted and accessed through digital presentation. New technologies provide teaching and learning with promising possibilities; and they make teaching and learning more flexible and more creative. The key word for this kind of design is *interactivity*.

An audience uses devices such as a keyboard, mouse, or touch screen to access information. Most of the designs involve two or more media components and support highly interactive features. Multimedia interactive instruction provides comprehensive activities of reading, writing, listening, and classifying in a multi-sensory environment.

Designing interactive instructional materials is challenging yet rewarding in terms of a learner's internal motivation. Many factors should be considered in the design procedure because interactive instructional design needs to deal with large amounts of information. The designer should carefully structure the information and establish an effective, logical interrelationship and *hierarchy*. It is necessary to make the navigation of the instructions as easy as possible. *Consistency* in text, color, shape, and other aspects of interface design is very important.

In interactive instructional design, the use of visuals – graphics, charts, photos, animations, and video – has been a great concern. Appropriate use of visuals can facilitate learning by giving the audience opportunities to perceive, accept, recall, analyze, synthesize, and memorize.

Listed on this page are some interactive instructional designs that are featured on the Web. "*Web-based Teaching Portfolio*," is a presentation that introduces how to use web-based teaching portfolio as a teaching tool in order to enhance classroom teaching. "*Office XP Key Concepts Illustrated*," is an interactive training suite that gives users hands-on experiences in learning software applications. And "*PC Treasure Box*" features a web-based computer literacy course designed for users who need basic knowledge of computers.

Empty and Full

What does "empty" mean? What does "full" mean? How does a pair of contradictions in Chinese philosophy generate endless discussions? How is it, then, further applied to graphic design?

Emptiness and fullness include both the compositional considerations and the meaning a composition can provide to the audience, as well as the response from audience. Emptiness and fullness supplement each other and correspond to each other, thus demonstrating the relationship of *interdependence*. The *contrast* of emptiness and fullness, in its obvious form, is when you look at a design and find that some areas contain neither images nor text, whereas some areas do contain some images and text.

A graphic designer's intention is to create productions that represent character, quality, and feeling. Within a design, the arrangement of *space* is the most important aspect of thought. Empty spaces, just like shapes and colors, are also *design elements*. We must understand that graphic design is not a still condition, but a creative procedure that involves positive participation from both designers and audience. Empty space offers potentials for a designer and audience alike to create a new space in which the communication needs are fulfilled. This deliberately arranged empty space, in interaction with other spaces, unifies the design and the audience, thus making aesthetic appreciation possible. Therefore, empty is not only the empty area in a two-dimensional space, but also the *space* for prolonged *imagination* and *association*. That's why a design that contains very few design elements can give audience a huge amount of information, but a design that lets design elements occupy every single square inch of space might result in the audience's feeling lost.

The *involvement* of emptiness in fullness and vice versa also shows how *fullness* supports *emptiness* and presents a more interesting aspect of this pair of contradictions. Shapes, colors, text, and any other full spaces help the designer achieve the highest artist conception, *fullness*, in order to allow the audience to enter the highest *appreciation* status, *emptiness*. It is just a sense of the highest *unity* or Tao — the natural flow, the nothing, the inner harmony, the contemplation, and the enlightenment. Eventually, emptiness is filled with meaning and it is full of meaning. But the meaning is implied and is made possible with the designer's attempt to express a sense of poetic *rhythm*.

Graphic design is *functional*, but it shouldn't be regarded as solely utilitarian and without any aesthetic values. Actually, design history has already demonstrated that good designs are appreciated generation after generation even when their original, practical purpose is not important at all.

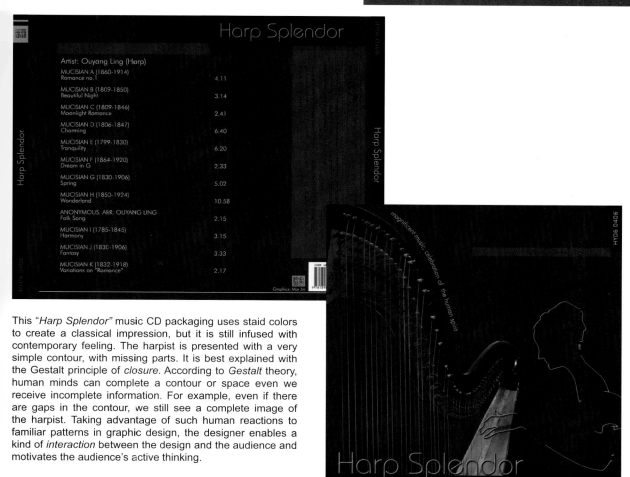

Artist: Ouyang Ling (Harp)

MUCISIAN A (1860-1914) Romance no.1	4.11
MUCISIAN B (1809-1850) Beautiful Night	3.14
MUCISIAN C (1809-1846) Moonlight Romance	2.41
MUCISIAN D (1806-1847) Charming	6.40
MUCISIAN E (1799-1830) Tranquility	6.20
MUCISIAN F (1864-1920) Dream in G	2.33
MUCISIAN G (1830-1906) Spring	5.02
MUCISIAN H (1850-1924) Wonderland	10.58
ANONYMOUS. ARR. OUYANG LING Folk Song	2.15
MUCISIAN I (1785-1845) Harmony	3.15
MUCISIAN J (1830-1906) Fantasy	3.33
MUCISIAN K (1832-1918) Variations on "Romance"	2.17

Graphics: Mai Jin

Harp Splendor

magnificent music celebration of the human spirit

Harp Splendor

This *"Harp Splendor"* music CD packaging uses staid colors to create a classical impression, but it is still infused with contemporary feeling. The harpist is presented with a very simple contour, with missing parts. It is best explained with the Gestalt principle of *closure.* According to *Gestalt* theory, human minds can complete a contour or space even we receive incomplete information. For example, even if there are gaps in the contour, we still see a complete image of the harpist. Taking advantage of such human reactions to familiar patterns in graphic design, the designer enables a kind of *interaction* between the design and the audience and motivates the audience's active thinking.

On page 37, you read about basic considerations of data CD packaging. This section discusses *music CD packaging* design with respect to the artistic value of music. Music CD packaging design, to a great extent, is a visual explanation of the music.

Appropriate explanations of music in CD packaging design can motivate the audience's desire to purchase the CD. Many people from the audience are highly visual-driven. Therefore, good packaging designs give an audience a deep primary impression, and it often becomes part of a collection for its own values.

Music is an abstract art and it is a very challenging task to visualize it. The composition, the melody, the harmony, the rhythm, and the timbre of a particular piece of music and the style of a particular musician can not be reproduced in visual media. So the visual explanation is an original, creative work of the graphic designer.

Simple and Complex

Keep it simple — this is a piece of advice that many new designers receive, because intricate compositions might eventually generate chaos in design. But how simple a design should be? And how "simple" is considered simple? Unfortunately, there are no standards or formula for answering those questions.

A design might be too complex if it has unnecessary images, inconsistent colors and styles, or jam-packed *space*. A design might be too simple if it has inactive spaces, inadequate images and text, or dull colors and shapes. In order to unveil complex concepts to the audience through simple ways, designers need to know how far to go and when to stop.

Effective designs break complex ideas down into component parts. Instead of overwhelming the audience with information, the designer "unfolds" each part of the design *hierarchically*; therefore, it can keep the audience's attention from straying while it introduces the concept of the design. In those designs, visual and verbal elements are organized in a good *hierarchy*, and the most important part is *emphasized* to create a focal *point* in order to grab the audience's attention. Also, certain shapes and colors are *repeatedly* used to indicate the relationships between pieces of information, following the *Gestalt similarity* principle. Simplicity does not mean effortless layout, but means careful arrangement. That's why some designs have engaged in much greater sophistication and complexity than some simple ones. They have all the stylistic and fabulous details, and can still keep the *whole* of the design while communicating effectively.

Graphic design principles of balance, unity, contrast, proportion, harmony, rhythm, and emphasis can be followed to help concept presentation. Visual perception theories, such as the Gestalt theory, can help in making complex messages and ideas easy for understanding and retaining. For example, a designer can put related *visual* and *verbal* elements close in position, following the principle of being in *proximity*. Gestalt psychology indicates that when related objects are put together, the human mind tends to perceive them as a coherent pattern or group. Therefore, in a layout, visually related items should be intellectually related items. If they are not intellectually related, they should not be visually related in the layout.

Let's take "*Visual Literacy*," the magazine design on page 53 as an example. The title, "Visual Literacy as Function and Action," is displayed in three lines, together with the illustration. The line of "as Function and Action" is emphasized with large and decorative fonts in order to gain attention. Although the title is in three parts and has different styles, the three parts are visually close enough in the space for readers to acquire all the information of the title. The strategy of creating the title is more effective than the actually placing the title; a long line without the emphasis on certain words would not have been very effective.

Magazines are multi-page, informative periodicals that feature articles and related illustrations. A wide range of topics can be covered by magazines, including news, entertainment, politics, academics, home and lifestyle, or men and women. Magazines are commonly published weekly, monthly, bi-monthly, or quarterly.

Typical components of a magazine consist of cover, editorial information, contents table, featured articles, departments, highlights, reviews, reports, advertisements, and editor's notes. In today's market, magazines often are required to have attractive covers, interesting and short articles, as well as eye-pleasing and colorful illustrations.

Although each issue of a magazine is different from the others, a formal *grid* system is usually applied to keep *consistency* among all issues. The grid system ties all the different issues together, and therefore helps in establishing the visual image of the magazine. A grid is useful in designing both the page layouts of magazines and the *magazine covers*. One-column, two-column, and three-column grids are among the typical choices, according to the needs in arranging paragraphs and illustrations. One of the challenges of magazine design is that magazines generally address a large audience. Readers of the magazines not only have different demographic backgrounds, but also have a diversity of *appreciation interest*. Successful magazine designs are able to meet the audience's needs, and at the same time, foster particular *appreciation interests*.

"Visual Education" magazine features articles and instructions of visual communication. The "*Visual Literacy*" section uses a slightly different grid to design the layout of the facing pages. The left page uses an informal, three-column grid system in which one column is narrower than the other columns. Except for a few quotes, the narrow column it is almost empty. This *scholar's margin* creates a dynamic white space in the page and emphasizes the title of the article.

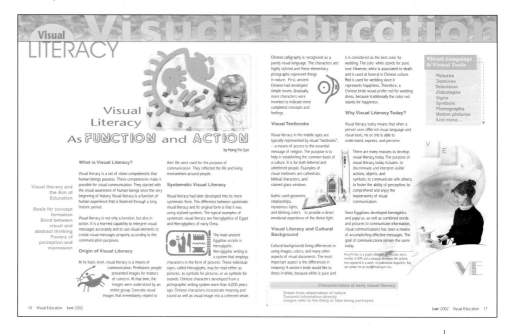

*U*nity is the sense that guides an audience to recognize a design as a whole. In a design that has unity, the visual elements are related to one another and are efficiently tied together in a meaningful way; therefore, the cohesion of the design is maintained. *Variety* introduces the necessary alteration into the design, and thus creates a dynamic impression. Without variety, a composition would be exceedingly dull and boring. Viewing the design examples in this book, you will find that each one is a synthesis of rhythmic lines, harmonious colors, consistent typographic attributes, and identical artistic style. Among those, a predominant color scheme has considerable significance.

In order to achieve unity, designers usually follow the principle of repetition in various aspects of a design. *Repetition* principle means that the designer makes use of the same or similar color, shape, font, line, grid, style, and so forth repeatedly in a design, so as to give the audience a consistent and smooth impression of the oneness of the design. A design that has unity can help the audience follow ideas and understand the message the design wishes to convey.

Achieving unity is especially critical in multi-page designs, such as magazines, web sites, and catalogs, because the designer will need to keep each page unique and interesting, but still maintain the entity and *whole* of the design. Through the analysis of the catalog design, *"Drawn to Charm"* on page 55, you will find that many methods of repetition can be applied to a design in order to achieve unity, but each adds variety to the design to avoid sameness.

First, the logo is repeatedly used on the cover and the inside pages. It appears on the cover as a functional, yet decorative button that ties up the cover. Starting from there, the audience will see that the logo serves as the background pattern for the inside pages. The logo, however, is produced in different colors in order to fit the special color scheme of each individual page.

Second, although each page has its special color scheme, type, and images, the *grid* system is repeatedly used for all the inside pages. The D-shaped logo is used for page *layout*. While the images of models appear along the vertical line and form a column, the product images are arranged along the curve line of the logo.

Third, the design avoids using visually confusing colors. The dominant colors, though having different hues for different pages, all fall into the *secondary* and *tertiary colors* and have similar *value* and *saturation*.

Unity and variety play a key figure in the wholeness of a design not only because they present the visual power but also because they are challenging arrangements of the design elements. Wholeness can be described in terms of unity and variety. The wholeness is able to unify all the details together while it is sufficiently integrated to maintain its variety. The prevailing balance between unity and variety encloses the superior harmony of compositions which provides our awareness of the profound meaning of graphic design.

A *catalog* contains information about products or services in the form of a booklet or pamphlet. It is a typical multi-page design that can be printed in one, two, or full color. The purpose of printed catalogs is to promote the products and increase sales, or to advertise services.

Most catalogs contain descriptions, illustrations, prices, and order information of listed product or services. Also, they vary in size and paper quality, depending on purpose and budget. Product name, model, dimension, size, or book title, author, description, price, and so forth will need to be included in order to give the audience detailed information.

A good combination of visual and verbal is the key of an effective catalog design. *Consistency* in using color, type, style, and grid can help to generate visual impact as well as professionalism. Legibility should be ensured in order to make it easy for the audience to obtain information. You can try to achieve *unity* in typography by limiting number of *type families,* but to add *variety* by changing type properties such as *type style* and sizes, as well as colors.

You will also need to make decisions on whether to introduce products individually or as groups. Showing products individually is to "spell-out" each product and can give the audience a deep impression.

The catalog design, "*Drawn to Charm*" repeatedly uses the D-shape of the logo for page *layout.* Look at how the products and related information are arranged to follow the curve line on the solid color of their backgrounds. Shadows lay stress on product images.

Regularity and Anomaly

You might have heard of the stories of some artists who found the beauty of abstract art by looking at their paintings upside down. They had just been overwhelmed and inspired by the deep impression that the upside-down painting gave them. As a graphic designer, how can you give your audience a new way of seeing art? Or how do you give the audience a striking impression through special visual strategies?

The main point here is to let images appear in an exceptional way, or what is referred to as a method of *anomaly*. Also, in graphic design efforts, a number of techniques can be used for anomaly, some of which involve using visual surprises or even a shock, whereas others are achieved by repeatedly using similar or identical patterns to make an impression of normality, while emphasizing one unique pattern at some point of the design.

We can try to use the *Gestalt* principle of similarity to support our effort in creating innovative designs through the method of anomaly. *Similarity*, in addition to the other Gestalt principles such as figure/ground, continuation, closure, and proximity, is yet another principle of visual grouping. It suggests that the human mind tends to perceive similar visual qualities, such as a group or pattern. If we extend the meaning of similarity to the achievement of *unity* in graphic design, we will find that color, grid, texture, shape, size, color, or any of the other *elements of design* can all be used as identifiers of objects. Similarity is also useful if we need regularity in design. The potential of the similarity principle lies at the point that we can create an intentional dissimilarity in the group, that is, anomaly.

The business *gifts* designs on page 57 shows a simple way of using anomaly to make the t-shirt gift appealing. It is to select the object or shape that is to be used over and over, or the *motif*. Both *proximity* and similarity related principles are followed for visual grouping. The regularity is accomplished. However, despite the audience's accustomed way of viewing the pattern, variations of color, shape, and value happen. That result thoroughly turns the nature of the visual experience to one that is challenging and inspiring.

Anomaly techniques increase the chances for viewers to pay attention to the design, resulting in high visual interest. These techniques are needed for many design tasks. However, anomaly can not be overused because overusing it might make a design appear unpersuasive. No matter how talented, a designer cannot let every single *detail* of a design be unique, because a detail seems unique only when it is on a normal background, surrounded by normal patterns.

From a macro point of view, anomaly can create a focal point of time. From a micro point of view, anomaly can create a *focal point* of a single artwork. It can call specific attention to some points of the design that need *emphasis*.

Business gifts involve virtually unlimited design areas in addition to graphic design. To create these requires cooperation with designers from other areas, such as product design. What can serve as business gifts? Apparel – T-shirts and jackets; office supplies – pens, desk planners, sticky notes, mouse pads, staplers, and staple removers; travel and outdoor gear – umbrellas, sun screen, sun visors, and beach balls; and countless other things.

From the design view, all business gifts belong to the effort of promoting a company or an organization through visual communication. The primary considerations of designing business gifts are the company or organization *logo,* standard color, and standard font.

Business gifts can be directly or indirectly related to the products of a company. For instance, a computer company may be giving away mouse pads or a fashion company may be giving away sun screen or lipstick. Some business gifts are unique and personalized, or designed for special events.

These business gifts are designed for the Rhythm·East Carolyin Fashion Studio. Notice that the logo appears on each individual item – the t-shirt, the umbrella, and the water bottle. A folding umbrella made with nylon fabric is a favorite gift for the customers. It uses the logo and standard color, but it can add some varieties to emphasize the studio's image. The t-shirt design shares some common characteristics with the umbrella design, but it includes some amusing aspects in order to create a relaxed feeling. The polycarbonate water bottle with a translucent screw off lid is at once functional and decorative.

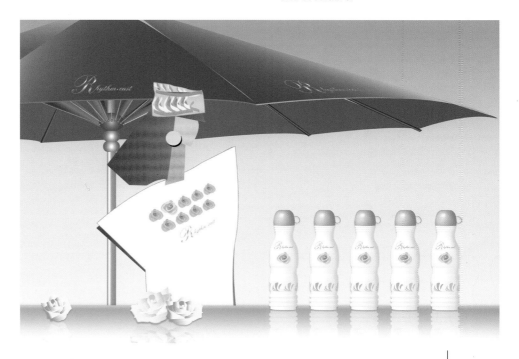

Certainty and Fortuity

The relationship between an intentional pursuit and a fortuitous outcome is often a complex one. Sometimes, a rational consensus on comprehensive conceptions of the meaning and value of design is not expected. In the process of creation, it, at times, is the intuitive process that plays a vital role. In literature, writers can write with ease and let the pen flow wherever the mind goes; and in fine art, artists can paint unconsciously and allow direct expression to come out with automatism. What are the possibilities for graphic designers?

Graphic design *procedure* does support fortuity and certainty, two elements that it requires in order to exist. Certainty involves the overview of the design problem, research of design solutions, analysis of the audience, creation of the layouts, and the use of images and type. Fortuity is covered by on-going creative activities while inspecting the design problem, examining design solutions, analyzing the audience, creating the layouts, and using images and type.

In the very early design stages, *brainstorming* plays a very important role. As an individual or as a group is developing thoughts and generating ideas, brainstorming allows anyone or any group of people to let the ideas flow in an easy fashion and in a relatively short period of time. *Association, imagination,* affection, synaesthesia, and imagery can be involved in brainstorming. On occasions, a sudden apprehension might determine the whole outcome of the design.

The brainstorming activity is usually accompanied by, or results in, visualizations referred to as thumbnail sketches. *Thumbnail sketches* are where the designer produces an initial visual structure of the design. This usually includes a series of very small and simple drawings, plus descriptions in words. Thumbnail sketches will enable you to visualize your ideas and will also be able to provide a clear record of the development of your ideas. Stream of thought and feeling, free association, and interweaving of reality and illusion can all occur in the thumbnail sketching procedure. Sometimes, the designer simply captures a spontaneous impression of an observed objects, scene, or event. However, the predominant feature appears as a deliberation.

Computer graphic programs also play an important role in fortuity or the unexpected effect of a design. In using tools, such as airbrush, gradient, or filters and effects, designers usually will need to try different tool or filter attributes before the desired effect is achieved. This process contains a great potential for discovering unanticipated outcomes. For example, while creating the digital imaging "*Space*" on page 59, the designer was trying to generate a feeling of the brilliant and changeful space of music. Factors such as the brightness of a certain color, the direction of a certain line, and the degree of a certain curve, determined the process of visualization of this feeling. The interesting thing is, a large part of these factors are influenced by the unexpected effects during the use of computer graphic programs.

To sum up, certainty ensures the realization of a well-planned design; and fortuity promises flexibility and unexpected results in design.

This *digital imaging* design, "*Space*," incorporates digital photos as well as images created with vector-based and bitmap-based graphics software applications. It uses various painting tools, drawing tools, and filters among the software features to generate a fascinating play of light.

There are some other factors you need to pay attention to when working in the digital world, in addition to the factors discussed in other sections of this book. For example, resolution and image size should be decided before you start a new design.

Resolution is related to the quality or fineness of images, and it is measured by the number of *pixels per inch* (ppi). And because images will be displayed via different media, different ways of determining resolution will be used. When you are designing a full color work such as a brochure, the resolution of your file needs to be set to at least 300 or 350 ppi. When you are designing web graphics or other graphics to be displayed on screen, a resolution of 72 to 96 ppi is enough because those are what most screens can display. *Pixels per inch* also relates to *screen resolution*; that is, the number of pixels on the entire screen. Figure A demonstrates how two 1″x1″ images, although the same size when printed on a page, appear differently on screen. The larger one has a resolution of 350 ppi and will be printed in higher image quality; the smaller one has a resolution of 72 ppi and will be printed in lower image quality. You might also have heard another kind of resolution, *dots per inch* or *dpi*. It refers to how many dots a printer can print within a square inch and it is not to be confused with ppi.

New designers will often worry about the jaggedness of a graphic or text in digital design, the alias. It is caused by the limitations of the resolution of a screen. A technique, called *anti-alias* technique, is available to smooth the rough edges or aliasing when you are working on digital images.

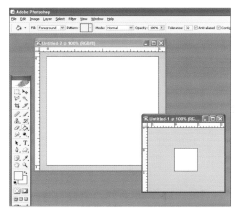

Figure A. Resolution

Contemporary and Traditional

When we are fascinated with any good design work, we also wish to know what lies behind those innovative ideas, tasteful arrangements, and superb techniques. Why do some contemporary designs give us a sense of historical depth? Why are some traditional designs still inspiring contemporary designers? Why do some contemporary designers have a desire to look back into the tradition? And why are some designs using traditional motifs even if they still look contemporary?

To answer these questions, we need to recognize that graphic design is based on the interweaving of historical accumulations and new experiences. Graphic design is not an isolated phenomenon of human history; and a designer is not an isolated individual within a culture. Regardless of what kind of designs involved, *history* is everywhere. History affects the design procedure when a designer is looking for solutions to a specific design task.

Contemporary concepts turn out designs that are current, or modern, and a continuing inheritance of culture from *tradition* formulate the fundamental principles. It is only with the background of accumulation supplied by *tradition* that the idea of being *contemporary* makes any sense at all. Arts of various major periods of Western and Eastern civilizations have enriched and developed humanistic expression and visual communication tools. The historical vision brings us back to the hieroglyphs and illustrated manuscripts created by Ancient Egyptians; the visual language of Chinese pictographs and calligraphy; illuminated manuscripts of Medieval Europe; the invention of photography; the contribution of *Art Nouveau* to the realm of design; the visually striking posters during World War I; the involvement of pure visual forms for harmony by De Stijl (The Style) movement in the Netherlands; the effort to unify arts and industry of the Bauhaus school; the contribution of the International Typographic Style to structured information presentation; and the innovative designs of the information age, with digital tools.

Also, not only are graphic design productions themselves both contemporary and traditional, but the techniques and tools are both contemporary and traditional so they can develop and grow. Usually, graphic designers can be inspired by other traditional or contemporary designers while shaping new styles and compositions.

task of catching the attention of potential readers. The placement of text and use of images should reflect the content of the book. In a book jacket design solution, you have to pay special attention to the binding style of the book because it is related closely to other issues, such as cover stock, paper weight, and trim size.

The cover art of the jacket is an illustration that uses different *shapes*, especially geometric shapes and organic shapes. Circles, squares, triangles, and rectangles, are simple *geometric shapes* identified by mathematical methods and used in design. For example, the early ancient *Greek vase painting* style used many repeated geometric shapes. *Organic shapes* are free forms that come from nature. Plants, marine echinoderms, and organs of the body can all be used to create organic shapes through free imagination.

A *book jacket* is a wrapper or packaging, usually made from paper, for a hardback book to keep the book clean. In addition to considerations, such as author, subject matter, image use, and font selection, book jacket design involves more technical considerations than regular *book cover* designs. Because a book jacket has more components than a book cover, fitting the book exactly is a more challenging work for jacket designers.

A typical book jacket, like a normal book cover, has both front and back covers, as well as a spine. What is special for a book jacket is the flaps – an inside front cover flap and an inside rear cover flap. The whole book jacket is one design, and the flaps are folded around 3 inches. The design of book jackets, just like that of book covers, should focus on the

The book jacket for "*The Folk Art in Southern China*" has a glowing look that designates one of the characteristics of folk art – brilliant color – and that also designates a color of happiness in Chinese culture – the color red. The front cover of this jacket includes the book title, author's name, and an illustration. The back cover of the jacket contains the book title, author's name, publishing company name, and barcode. The spine emphasizes the title, author, and publishing company. Notice how the inside front cover flap presents promotional information to prospective readers and the inside rear cover flap introduces the author in detail.

Great designs have a timeless quality because they have recorded the cultural life of a society. They have the capability of evoking memories, inspiring innovations, giving exciting feelings, and motivating creative activities. The point is that the justification of eternity in graphic design does not have the force of a proof either in objective terms or in terms of a universal subjective need. Graphic design is a functional art, but it always has its spiritual aspects. Infinite beauty is achieved through the designer's *creative imagination*. When a design is empowered with universal appeal, it transmits the innermost significance of the design.

Read graphic design *history* and look at the masterpieces. You and the designers might not belong to the same period of time, but there is something in their designs that moves you. The event announced in a poster or a product presented in an advertisement now is too far away from your life; however, the beauty of the design adds light to your life. Or, the design is using a language that you don't speak, but the visual impact of the design on you is strong.

In this context the discussion of infinity might well be understood generally in terms of art, life, and spirit. Something in design can be sensed, but can not be explained with words. We find ourselves enjoying the art, the emotion, the power, and, the

infinity. We are experiencing the timeless beauty of graphic design. And we can understand this timeless beauty only if we understand that graphic design is an entity composed of all its cultural, religious, philosophical components – humanistic expression.

Although graphic designs are created at a certain time, in a specific cultural context, and are used for a limited time period, the beauty of design gives the audience an inspiration that lasts through the ages. By the means of a designer's personal artistic language and style, the audience is affected by an artistic impact of forms and meanings of the design. The ethereal feeling leads the audience toward an artistic atmosphere in which the noise of this world dims down greatly. No one should be surprised, then, that there is an infinite quality of graphic design which bridges the past and the future, and bridges the Nature and the soul – a feast for the spirit.

A *magazine* is a periodical that has a theme or subject matter. Entertainment, travel, fashion, sports, finance, food, and nutrition can all serve as the subject matter of a magazine. A magazine can feature articles, stories, pictures, or other items.

The *magazine cover*, just like a book cover, plays a significant role in magazine design. Every magazine should have its own unique style in order to stand out in a very competing market. A unique style reflects the past, present, and future of a magazine.

Magazine cover design for every issue is the key to attract potential readers. The designer must be aware of the trend, must know the audience, and must use images and text that reflect the content. The most common methods of cover design include, but are not limited to, novel layout, contrast of color, montage, and even a shock. An individual designer has his/her own philosophy of establishing the magazine's unique style.

The cover of "*Carolyin Music Instruments,*" though using classic images, yields a very modern look. It is truly simple in many aspects and it explains the everlasting appeal of music. Its logo ingeniously replaces the letter "u" with a harp, thus enhancing the subject. It is clean and well-defined, and it has built an integrated brand name. The promotion image for the featured musician, "in my heart, in my soul," demonstrates the *expressional* aspect of graphic design.

Summary

Graphic design is a kind of art that is essentially expected to minimize expression. However, it tends to eliminate meaning from the designer's personal artistic traits. Only by analyzing the conceptual part of the design, can we present a more balanced picture of graphic design. It answers the question of "what you think" by seeing graphic design. It is the visual force and aesthetic appeal of graphic design that attract people, impact people, and move people. Sections in this chapter help designers gain a broader view of the depth of graphic design from conceptual aspects.

Content Map

References

Livingston, A. and Livingston, I. (1998). *The Thames and Hudson Dictionary of Graphic Design and Designers*. New York, NY: Thames and Hudson.

Arnheim, R. (1974) *Art and Visual Perception: A Psychology of the Creative Eye*. Berkeley and Los Angeles, CA: University of California Press.

Crozier, R. (1994). *Manufactured Pleasures: Psychological Responses to Design*. New York, NY: Manchester University Press.

Gombrich, E. H. (1989). *Art and Illusion: A Study in the Psychology of Pictorial Representation*. (2nd Ed.) New York, NY: Pantheon Books.

Kemp, M. (2000). (Ed.) *Oxford History of Western Art*. Oxford; New York, NY: Oxford University Press.

Kleiner, F. S., Mamiya, C. J., and Tansey, R. G. (2001). (11th Ed.) *Gardner's Art Through the Ages*. Fort Worth, TX: Harcourt College Publishers.

Meggs, P. B. (1998). (3rd. Ed.) *A History of Graphic Design*. New York, NY: John Wiley & Sons, Inc.